NatWest Business Handbook

This series has been written by a team
experience and are still actively invo
the small business.

If you are running a small business or are thinking of setting up your own business, you have no time for the general, theoretical and often inessential detail of many business and management books. You need practical, readily accessible, easy-to-follow advice which relates to your own working environment and the problems you encounter. The NatWest Business Handbooks fulfil these needs.

- They concentrate on specific areas which are particularly problematic to the small business.
- They adopt a step-by-step approach to the implementation of sound business skills.
- They offer practical advice on how to tackle problems.

The author

Thomas ('Tommy') Docherty is a taxation consultant to a number of small businesses and occasional adviser to small accountancy practices. He has over twenty years lecturing experience at both Glasgow Polytechnic and the Institute of Chartered Accountants of Scotland in Edinburgh. He is currently Chief Examiner in taxation for a major professional body and a member of the examination panel of another.

Other titles in this series

A Business Plan
Book-keeping and Accounting
Computerisation in Business
Employing and Managing People
Exporting
Financial Control
Franchising
Health and Safety
Hiring and Firing
Law for Small Businesses
Marketing Decisions
Purchasing for Profit
Running a Shop
Selling
Small Business Finance
Small Business Survival
Starting Up
Understanding VAT

To my wife Maureen for her help, encouragement and patience.

NatWest Business Handbooks

Taxation

2nd Edition

Thomas Docherty CA

Pitman Publishing
128 Long Acre, London WC2E 9AN
A Division of Longman Group UK Limited

First published in Great Britain in association with the National Westminster Bank, 1991
Second edition 1992, reprinted 1993

A CIP catalogue record for this book is available from the British Library.

ISBN 0 273 60030 3

Printed and bound in Singapore

The information in this book is intended as a general guide based upon the legislation at the time of going to press. Neither the Bank, its staff or the author can accept liability for any loss arising as a result of reliance upon any information contained herein and readers are strongly advised to obtain professional advice on an individual basis.

Contents

Preface

This book is aimed at the owners of small businesses and those who are considering starting a business for the first time. One of the difficulties which arise in discussing small businesses is just what is 'small' in this context. If you look at company law, you find that the criteria for establishing small company status include references to turnover not exceeding £2m and the number of employees not exceeding 50. For exemption from certain accounting standards the turnover figure goes up to £80m! If you were to ask a major accounting firm for a definition, they would possibly say a client whose fee was less than £5,000. In this book then, we are talking really small businesses, the kind run by one person or a married couple or a family and there are many more businesses of this kind in the UK than those which reach the above-mentioned thresholds.

The main objective of this book is to take most of the mystery out of tax and to answer the basic questions which, in the author's experience, are most commonly asked, i.e. 'What will I be taxed on?'; 'How is the tax calculated?' and 'When is the tax payable?'. Most business persons, particularly if they are successful, then get to the more interesting question: 'What can I do to reduce my tax bills?'. Much of the book is devoted to this aspect of tax with illustrations presented in a clear, easy-to-understand style.

Basic tax planning involves taking decisions about alternative courses of action, although it must be stressed that commercial wisdom must take precedence. The tax planning presented in this book involves considering the tax implications of these alternative courses of action to achieve a desired commercial objective.

There is no coverage of some of the more sophisticated, often artificial, methods of tax avoidance which have been the subject of challenge by the courts in recent years. Perhaps these may be risked once the business has grown beyond the thresholds indicated above!

Many taxation publications aimed at 'small' businesses often contain sections dealing with areas beyond the comprehension, or indeed the needs, of the average small business person. Such areas seem targeted at tax specialists and their inclusion often adds to the reader's initial confusion concerning taxation. This book hopefully avoids this pitfall. For instance, there is no detailed coverage of Share Option Schemes, since the intended readers of this book are not, at this stage, running businesses for which such schemes would be appropriate. Reading the book will not turn you into a taxation expert but it should prevent you making uninformed decisions and will put you in a position to ask relevant questions of your tax adviser. Those wishing to learn about the taxation treatment of multinational groups of companies will require to purchase another book!

All of the illustrations in the book reflect the changes in law introduced since the first edition was published, up to and including the two 1992 Finance Acts.

If you are reading this Preface in a bookshop, trying to make up your mind whether to buy the book, turn to the Appendix to Chapter 11 where there is a list of the taxation decisions covered throughout the various chapters. If you want the answers to any of these questions then this is the book for you!

Thomas Docherty
Milngavie, October 1992

1 Introduction

Terminology and sources of law □ Appendix 1 – Taxation implications of alternative business structures □ Appendix 2 – Creation of a Finance Act □ Appendix 3 – Administration of the UK tax system

To the individual starting out in business and to those currently in their first few years of self employment, tax and anything connected with it tends to be scary and shrouded in mystery. To the unprepared and uninformed the cascade of brown envelopes which descends on them tends to cause panic and occasionally results in the individual doing the worst possible thing – nothing! Most people in business get into difficulties, in relation to taxation matters, because they fail to respond to communications from the authorities and fail to seek any professional help until the position becomes desperate – like the bailiffs appearing at the door.

The principal objective of this book is to de-mystify, as far as possible, those areas of tax which experience suggests create the major problems for small businesses. It does not seek to turn those running small businesses into taxation experts but to create an awareness of the taxation implications of any course of action taken by them and to know which questions to ask and when.

The material will be presented in an order which corresponds to the normal progression of small businesses which is often as follows:

- **starting to trade as a sole trader**
- **assuming a partner (or later shedding a partner)**
- **forming a company to take over the existing business.**

Each of these events has important taxation implications and there are certain matters which affect all businesses, regardless of the type of business being run. Examples of these would be the Pay As You Earn system (PAYE) and National Insurance Contributions (NIC).

Value Added Tax will not be covered in any detail and readers are referred to the other publication in this series.

In the following chapters the book will attempt to answer the following questions:

- **What is tax paid on? What are 'profits' for tax purposes?**
- **How is the income assessed? This question is of critical importance in a new or a ceasing business.**
- **When is the tax charged paid? Are appeals possible?**
- **What happens if a partner is taken on? Should a spouse be a partner? This latter question assumes added importance in the light of independent taxation of married couples which commenced on 6 April 1990.**
- **Should a company be formed? If so, what is the tax position of the company and the owners? How does it differ from a sole trader or partnership? (See Appendix 1 to this chapter.)**
- **What action must be taken if employees are taken on?**
- **What if the business makes a loss?**
- **What other taxes can arise?**

The progression of the book will be particularly helpful to those about to start a business. Those already in business can pick up the progression at the point they now find themselves. Perhaps they could look at earlier chapters and find out where they went wrong!

It may be useful to readers to be aware of the structure of the administration of taxation in the UK (excluding VAT) and to appreciate the manner in which tax legislation comes into being. Appendices 2 and 3 show the structure and process.

Throughout the book any tax calculations are based on the rates and allowances introduced in the 1992 Finance Act.

Two final cautionary notes

If, as a result of reading this book, you become aware that any proposed action by you could have important tax implications, then always consult your tax adviser **before** you take the action. For example, if you decide to cease trading (or convert an existing business to a company) and do so without seeking advice on the timing, you will be upset to learn later that a different date could have saved you, quite legitimately, several thousands of pounds of tax. It is most often too late to change the situation, especially if you have disposed of the business premises! You should always bear in mind that, as a general rule, commercial considerations should always take precedence over taxation implications – you must not allow the 'tax tail' to wag the 'commercial dog'. There may, however, be two ways in which to achieve a commercial objective and obviously one should consider which way is the most tax efficient. If the sole approach is to reduce tax by actions which have no commercial motives then recent decisions in the courts would suggest that such an approach may not be successful in reducing the tax burden as intended.

Terminology and sources of law

As everyone is aware, on each Budget day the Chancellor of the Exchequer announces the tax changes which will apply for the ensuing tax year and these are contained in a Finance Bill. After being debated in Parliament and being considered in committee, the provisions, containing any amendments made, are published as the Finance Act (FA). (See Appendix 2.) After a period of years, the various Finance Acts are consolidated into the Income and Corporation Taxes Act (ICTA 1988). This last took place in 1988 and all references to section numbers in this book will be to this Act unless otherwise stated. In keeping with the non-technical approach adopted in this text, such references will be kept to a minimum.

The administration of the UK tax system is shown in Appendix 3 and you will notice the references to the general and special commissioners of the Inland Revenue. It is to these bodies that a dissatisfied taxpayer may appeal. The procedure is dealt with in Chapter 3.

The income tax year runs from the 6 April one year to the 5 April the following year and the year to 5 April 1993 is described as the tax year 1992/93. Alternative descriptions are often applied such as 'the fiscal year' or the 'year of assessment'. They all mean the same thing. These double-barrelled names have no relevance for limited companies which are dealt with under different arrangements.

The rates of income tax and the allowances and reliefs granted to individual taxpayers for the tax year 1992/93 are shown in the Appendix on p. 159.

Appendix 1 – Taxation implications of alternative business structures

	Limited Company	*Sole Trader*
1. Loss relief	Locked into company. May be relieved against previous three years' income at any point within the company's life	Available against taxpayer's other income and gains. Loss can be used against previous three years' income in the case of a new business (s.381)
2. Payment of tax	Paid nine months later	Interval can be 20 months (not in a new business)
3. Capital gains	Element of double taxation – once in company – again when shares are sold	Taxed only once. Personal exemption £5,800.
4. NIC	Must be paid for directors (monthly). Employer's share 10.4% of wages	Self employed contributions are much lower
5. Withdrawal of funds	Attracts immediate tax – dividends = ACT – salaries = PAYE + NIC	Attracts no immediate tax
6. Benefits and perks	Rather easier to provide. Can be used as a shelter from NIC	Owners taxed on private use element
7. Rates of tax	Small company rate – profits up to £250,000 – 25%. Marginal rate 35% (see Chapter 7).	20% on first £2,000, 25% on next £21,700. Highest rate 40% above £23,700.
8. Unscrambling	Not easy to extricate oneself – company must be wound up.	No major problems in extrication.

The detail involved in each of the above areas will be dealt with in the following chapters and, in Chapter 7, an illustration, using figures to make the comparison, appears.

Appendix 2 – Creation of a Finance Act

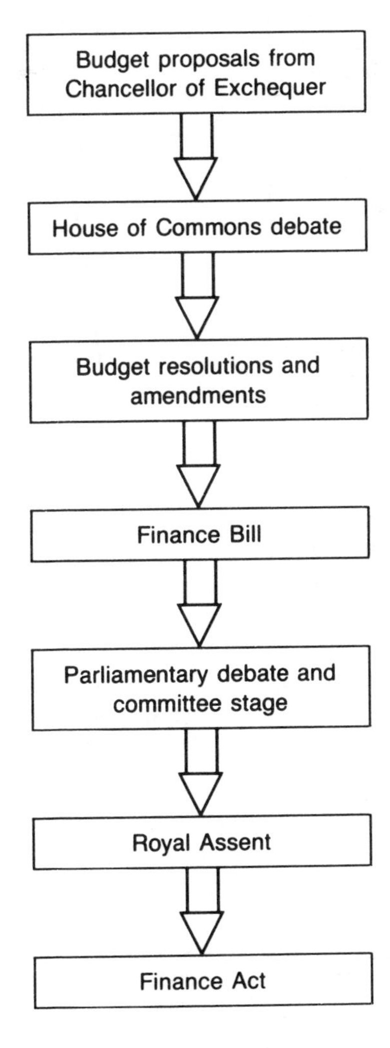

Appendix 3 – Administration of the UK tax system

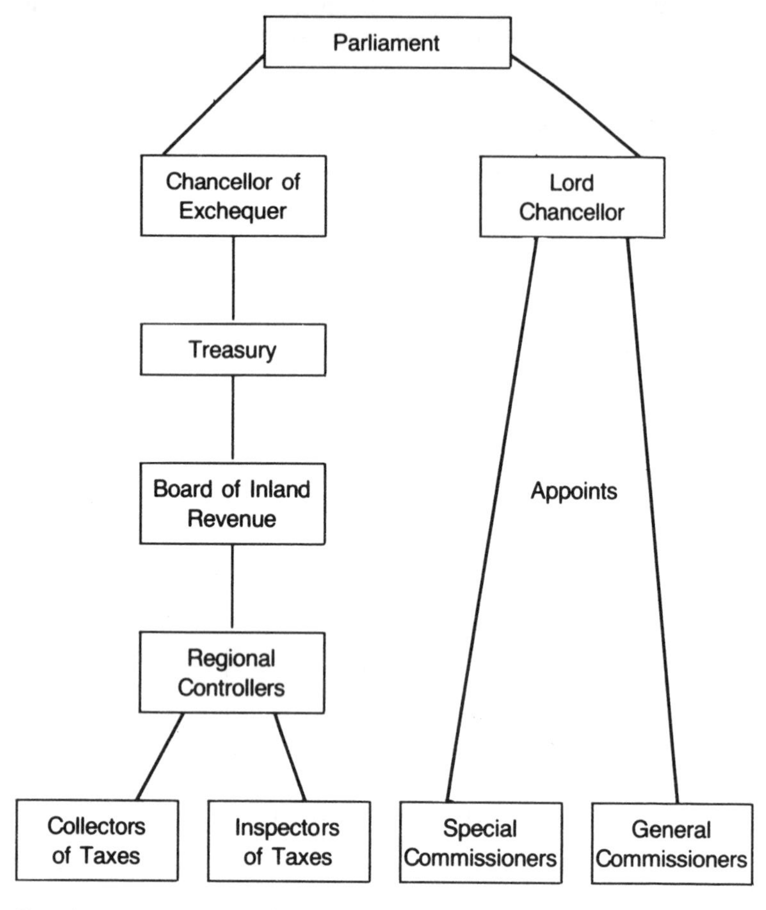

For the vast majority of taxpayers, their contact with the tax system will be via the Inspector of Taxes responsible for the area where they live or where their business premises are located. In most cases agreement on the taxation liability will be reached, often through a professional adviser, with the local (or district) Inspector. Where agreement cannot be reached, the taxpayer may have his case considered by either the general or special commissioners – which will depend on the nature of problem. (See Chapter 3.)

The Collector's role is fairly straightforward. You just send him your money! Occasionally problems do arise, such as a final demand appearing after you have paid in full or where the tax involved is still under appeal. In most cases such difficulties can be quickly resolved.

2 Business profits

The Schedular System □ What are trading profits? □ Allowable expenditure □ Rules for adjusting profits for tax purposes □ Adjustment of profits □ Schedule DI – Adjustment of profits

The Schedular System

For taxation purposes in the UK, different types of income are classified into what are known as **Schedules** some of which are further sub-divided into **Cases**. This is known as the Schedular System and its roots go back to the time when, for reasons of privacy, different departments of the Inland Revenue dealt with different types of income which a wealthy individual might have. The labels 'schedule' and 'case' have no important significance; they simply mean 'type' or 'sort'.

These reasons are no longer important and one Inspector of Taxes will deal with all aspects of a taxpayer's income in the tax district where the taxpayer resides or his business is located. There is, however, an important residue of the system in that depending on the schedule into which an item of income is classified will depend a number of aspects of how the income is treated for tax purposes:

- The method of **assessing** the income – i.e. the basis of assessment.
- The method of **measuring** the income; deductions which will be permitted.
- The date and method of **paying** the tax.

The schedules

	Type of income	Basis of assessment	Date paid
A	Income from land or property	Rents and premiums due in tax year	1 January in tax year
B	Occupation of woodlands on commercial basis	1/3 G.A.V. or on profits/losses	Ditto
(Effectively abolished from 6 April 1988.)			
C	Interest and dividends on Government stocks	Amounts received in tax year	Basic rate at source higher rate 1 December following tax year
D			
Cases I and II	Business profits	Adjusted profits for accounting year ending in preceding year of assessment	1 January in tax year – ½ 1 July after tax year – ½
Case III	Interest received gross – NSB interest	Income received in preceding tax year	1 January in tax year
Cases IV and V	Foreign income	Ditto (broadly)	Ditto
Case VI	All other income	Actual receipts in tax year	Ditto
E	Salaries and wages	Emoluments **paid** in tax year	PAYE
F	Dividends from UK	Actual receipts in tax year	Basic rate at source higher rate 1 Dec. following tax year

It is important to distinguish between the **tax year** or **fiscal year** (to 5 April) for which the income is **assessable** and **tax payable** and the **period for which or during which the income is received.** In taxation these are rarely the same.

The period for which or during which the income is received is known as the **basis period** and only in a minority of schedules does this coincide with the **fiscal year** under review.

In this chapter we consider what it is the Inland Revenue regard as taxable business profits. From the above table you will note that business profits are dealt with under Schedule D Cases I and II (strictly Case I deals with profits from trades and Case II covers profits from professions – the differences are small and no distinction is made in this book).

What are trading profits?

Most people in business, or about to start a business, will be familiar with a basic profit and loss account which shows the gross profit earned and then shows the various expenses of the business as deductions, finally arriving at the net profit (or loss) for the period.

In a minority of cases the figure of profit arrived at in this manner will be the trading income charged to income tax. In most cases however, this figure will require to be amended. This does not mean that the profit shown is 'incorrect' for accounting purposes; it requires adjustment because it may contain income items which the Inland Revenue do not regard as trading income or it may contain deductions which they regard as non-trading expenses. On the other hand, the profit might contain income items which do not look like trading income but the Revenue regards as such, or it may contain expenses items which do not look like trading expenses but are allowed as such by the Revenue.

The following are some examples of income items which the courts have decided are trading receipts and therefore taxable under Schedule D I, despite the fact that they do not look like trading receipts.

- **Compensation in excess of cost of repairs (loss of profits)**
  London and Thames Oil Wharves v. *Attwool*
- **Insurance recovery of value of timber destroyed in a fire**
  Green v. *Gliksten*
- **Bad debt recovered**
  Bristow v. *Dickenson*

- **Disposal of stock otherwise than through the trade to be included as a sale at market value,** i.e. when an owner takes goods for own use
  Sharkey v. *Wernher*

Allowable expenditure

While the taxing statutes make no attempt to define profit, there is some guidance given in Section 74, which sets out the principal items which are **disallowed** in arriving at the taxable profits of a trade. Section 74 states that:

> *'No sum shall be deducted in respect of disbursements or expenses not being money wholly and exclusively laid out or expended for the purpose of the trade, profession or vocation.'*

Main items disallowed by Section 74

- **Any personal (non-business) expenditure**
- **Any capital withdrawn from business (personal drawings/partners salaries)**
- **Any capital expenditure i.e. on or incidental to the acquisition of fixed assets (buildings, plant, equipment, etc.)**
- **Any debts unless specific bad debts**
- **Any sums which are recoverable under an insurance claim (the insurance recovery wipes out the expense)**
- **Any annual payment paid net of income tax. (Some loan interest or patent royalties)**

Clearly most businesses have many items charged in their Profit and Loss Account which are not dealt with in the Taxing Statutes and it has been left to the courts and Revenue practice to establish what is or is not allowed.

Some examples of items dealt with in decided cases

1. Major repairs

Costs expended to satisfy legal requirements or to bring a second-hand asset into working order – **are disallowed** – *Law Shipping* *case.* An example would be buying a building with no roof and putting a new roof on it.

Generally expenditure to bring a newly acquired, useable second-hand asset to a higher standard will be allowed – *Odeon Theatres case.* However, before embarking on such expenditure, advice should be sought. Where the expenditure is disallowed, it may be possible to claim capital allowances on the expenditure (see Chapter 4).

2. Interpretation of the wholly and exclusively concept

- Damages paid by a hotelier for injuries sustained by a guest – not incurred in earning profits or protecting assets – **disallowed** – *Strong* v. *Woodifield.*
- Misappropriation by directors – **disallowed** – *Bamford* v. *ATA Advertising.*
- Tax appeals (whether successful or not) – **disallowed** – *Allen* v. *Farquarson.* Note normal tax work is allowed.

Capital/revenue expenditure/repairs

As indicated above, capital expenditure on or incidental to the acquisition of **fixed assets** (including professional fees) is always **disallowed**. Revenue expenditure, i.e. all other expenditure on repairs, is allowed. However, there are grey areas in trying to distinguish between capital and revenue expenditure. The following items should be noted:

- **Improvement element in a repair – disallowed.** Examples would be:
    - (a) enlarging an existing door or window
    - (b) building a higher or thicker wall
    - (c) installing an improved roof.
- **No round sum provisions are allowed – only actual expenditure in period is allowed.**
- **Repairs by second-hand purchaser may or may not be allowed** – see case law above.

Other items normally allowed

- **Annual interest** – unless paid net of income tax
- **Advertising** – except for capital expenditure e.g. signs

- **Certain charitable subscriptions** – only local not national. Not to political parties.
- **H.P. interest** – but not capital repayments
- **Certain legal expenses** – in connection with trading activities or obligations as employer. Not in respect of capital expenditure or recovering non-trading debts. Allowable items include: Trade debt collection; normal tax work; rating valuation appeals; renewal of leases under fifty years and defending title to asset or protecting trading rights.
- **Losses** (see Chapter 6)
- **Pension contributions for staff or directors** – provided scheme has been approved.
- **Specific provisions** – e.g. for bad debts (see below)
- **Trade subscriptions**
- **Welfare expenses for staff** – e.g. sports clubs, local hospitals.
- **Some taxation** e.g. irrecoverable VAT but not income or corporation tax.

Items specifically allowed by statute

The following items are some of those specifically identified in statute as being allowed and override the 'wholly and exclusively' idea:

1. **Patent fees** – but not the cost of the patent
2. **Payments for technical education of staff**
3. **Any statutory redundancy payments to staff** plus up to **three** times this figure where there has been a cessation of a trade or part of a business
4. **Costs of raising loan finance** – provided the interest paid is deductible in arriving at the profits.
5. **Pre-trading expenditure incurred in the five years prior to start of trade** – provided it would have been allowed if incurred while trading. In a sole trader or partnership such expenditure is treated as an allowable loss occurring on the first day of trading (see losses later)
6. **Wages of workers seconded to charities.**
7. **Premiums on short leases (under 50 years)**
8. **Professional and trade subscriptions**
9. **Gifts to customers will be allowed as a deduction only where the gift:**

   - Costs less than £10 per person per year

- Contains a prominent advert
- Is not food, drink or tobacco.

The above restrictions do not apply to gifts to charities.

In general **all** expenditure on entertaining customers or suppliers is disallowed (prior to 15 March 1988 expenditure on foreign customers was allowed). Expenditure on entertaining staff – Christmas lunches, annual dances or outings – is allowed provided the expenditure does not exceed £50 per staff member. This is a concession allowed by the Revenue.

It is not unknown for individuals, especially students, to get the above ideas confused. Some have stated that expenditure on an office party would be allowed provided there was no food, drink or tobacco involved. This does not leave much to spend the money on! It has also been suggested to the author that, at a party, each member of staff would be allowed to drink up to £10 worth! One has visions of a Revenue official disguised as a waiter taking careful notes.

Bad debts adjustments

Where a customer fails to pay and the business takes all steps to recover the debt – use of solicitors etc. – the resultant bad debt will be allowed as a deduction against trading income. Where there is some uncertainty about the exact amount which may be recovered from a particular named customer, then an estimate of the potential loss will also be allowed as a deduction. However, where a trader simply makes an estimate of the probable bad debts, usually by taking a percentage of the outstanding debtors, then this amount would not be allowed as a deduction. Similarly, no deductions are permitted for non-trading bad debts e.g. loans to staff or customers. Additionally, any legal fees incurred in trying to recover such non-trading debts would also be disallowed.

Rules for adjusting profits for tax purposes

It must be remembered that the starting point for the adjustment process is the **net profit shown by the accounts**. The following rules then apply:

- **Any expense items disallowed must be ADDED to the existing profit (or deducted from a loss).**
- **Any expense item which is allowed must be left and NO ADJUSTMENT made.**
- **Any income item which is not taxable as TRADING income (or not taxable at all) must be DEDUCTED from the profit (or added to a loss).**
- **Any income item which is taxable as TRADING income must be left and NO ADJUSTMENT made.**

Recommended layout

	+	–
Profit/(Loss)	X	X
Expense items disallowed	X	
	X	
	X	
Income items not taxable		X
as trading income		X
		X
	XXX	XXX
	XXX	
Adjusted Schedule D I Profit	£XXXX	

Many people new to business have a peculiar approach to expenditure. They often ask the question, 'Can I spend money on my car, or my house, or my scuba diving equipment?'! The answer always is, of course, that they can spend their money on anything they like (provided they are not running the business as a limited company) – it is their own money! In some cases the expenditure will simply be treated as personal drawings (if it is not a business expense) and will not appear as a deduction in the profit and loss account. In other words, the foregoing rules do not *forbid* you to spend money on items which are disallowed for tax purposes, they just mean you *cannot charge them against tax.* It is, however advisable to use a separate bank account for personal expenditure.

At this stage we are considering only businesses being run as sole traders or partnerships. However, all of the foregoing rules apply, where appropriate, to limited companies also. When we come to consider companies (in Chapter 7) we will look at the minor differences which arise in arriving at a company's Schedule D I profit

– dividends; directors' salaries; and capital allowances. It will not be necessary to re-state the above rules and readers are recommended, when dealing with companies, to refer to this chapter.

There now follow two examples demonstrating the above adjustment rules:

- one dealing with a sole trader
- one dealing with a partnership.

Adjustment of profits

Case study illustration

Ben Dover, a sole trader, has been in business for many years as a fishmonger. His Profit and Loss Account for the year ended 31 December 1991 is shown below. Additional information concerning certain items is contained in the accompanying notes.

Profit and Loss Account

Note			*Note*		
(1)	Wages	£9,900		Gross profit	£38,000
	Heat & Light	750	(2)	Insurance recovery	380
(3)	Rent, rates & insurances	3,100		Rents received	500
	Telephones	360		Bank interest received	600
(4)	Repairs	950		Quantity rebate from suppliers	1,200
(5)	Motor expenses	1,800			
(6)	Bad debts	500			
	Patent fees	1,000			
	Loss on sale of van	900			
	Depreciation	1,500			
	NET PROFIT FOR YEAR	19,920			
		£40,680			£40,680

Notes:

1. Wages include £2,400 paid to Mr Dover's wife, Eileen, who works as a full time gutter.
2. The insurance recovery relates to stock damaged in a faulty freezer.
3. This figure includes £100 in respect of a personal life insurance premium for Mr Dover.
4. Repairs consist of:

replacement engine for van	£450
enlarging shop doorway	300
painting shop front	200

5. Motor expenses consist of:

van and lorry expenses	£1,100
private car expenses	700

The inspector of taxes has agreed that 40% of the car expenses are for non-business usage.

6. Bad debts comprise:

trade debts written off	£400
loan to employee written off	100

Solution to Ben Dover example

	+	–
Profit per accounts	£19,920	
Private insurance premium	100	
Enlarging door (capital expenditure)	300	
Motor expenses (private use – 40% × £700)	280	
Loan written off (non-trading debt)	100	
Loss on sale of lorry (capital item)	900	
Depreciation (capital item)	1,500	
Rents received (non-trading income – Schedule A)		£ 500
Bank interest (non-trading income – already taxed)		600
	23,100	1,100
	1,100	
Adjusted Schedule D I profit	£22,000	

Notes on items not adjusted:

- Wages – Wages paid to relatives are allowed provided the relative actually does the work, the wage is reasonable and the wages are actually paid. £2,400 seems a reasonable wage for a full time gutter!

- Heat and light; rent and rates and telephones are normal trading expenses – no adjustment.
- Repairs – Replacing engine is regarded as a normal repair. Had the van just been purchased this cost may have been regarded as capital expenditure and disallowed.
- Business motor expenses and trading debts are normal trading expenses.
- Patent fees are allowed by statute although they look like capital expenditure.
- The insurance recovery is regarded as trading income (*Green* v. *Gliksten*) and the quantity rebate is also trading income – no adjustment.
- Although rents received and bank interest are taxable in Mr Dover's hands, they are not trading income and must be removed at this stage.

Schedule D I – Adjustment of profits

Case study

The Gorbals Haute Couture Fashion Company is a long established business which has been carried on in partnership by the partners Fred Haute and Jimmy Couture.

From the following Profit and Loss Account for the year ended 31 December 1991 and the accompanying notes, you are required to compute the Schedule D I assessable on the firm for the tax year 1992/93.

Profit and Loss Account

Gross Profit			£31,385
Add,	Gain on sale of Fittings		120
	Discount received		280
	Insurance recovery – water damaged stock		300
			32,085
Less,	Expenses:		
Notes			
(1)	Staff salaries	£8,400	
	Rent, Rates & Insurances	2,500	
	Heating and Lighting	1,360	
(2)	Motor Upkeep & Repairs	2,580	
(3)	Subscriptions & Donations	130	

(4)	Entertainment Expenses			175	
(5)	Bad Debts			360	
(6)	Repairs			260	
(7)	Legal Expenses			180	
(8)	Sundry Expenses			340	
	Depreciation:	Motor Cars	£2,500		
		Fittings	1,800		
				4,300	
	Partners' Salaries:	Haute	4,500		
		Couture	3,000		
				7,500	
					28,085
NET PROFIT FOR THE YEAR					£ 4,000

Notes:

1. Staff salaries include £2,400 for Mr Haute's wife Sophie who works as a model.
2. Each partner has the use of a firm's car for which personal use has been agreed at 20%. Depreciation written off each of these cars during the year was £500. Repairs and servicing in respect of the partners' cars amounted to £1,600 for the year.
3. Subscriptions and donations consisted of:

Mr Haute's subscription to the Gorbals Ballet & Bingo Club	£ 25
Mr Couture's subscription the Gorbals Croquet club	30
Annual subscription to *Vogue Magazine*	40
Donation to local sports club used by staff	15
Donation to Red Cross	20
	£130

4. Entertainment expenses:

   This represents the cost of the firm's Christmas lunch for the staff of ten at the local Culture Club.
5. Bad debts:

Bad debts W/O	£160
Defalcation – cashier (he was fined in court)	80
Employee loan W/O	100
Increase in general provision	60
	£360

6. Repairs:

Repainting offices	£ 80
Repairs to fitting room	80
New display stands	100
	£260

7. Legal fees

Tax appeal (successful)	£ 70
Partner's divorce	50
Debt recovery	20
Employees' service contracts	40
	£180

8. All sundry expenses are allowable.

Solution to Gorbals Haute Couture example

		+	–
Profit per accounts		£4,000	
Gain on sale			£120
Motor upkeep – 20% × £1,600		320	
Subscriptions	Ballet & Bingo Club	25	
	Croquet Club	30	
	Red Cross	20	
Bad debts	Loan W/O	100	
	General provision increase	60	
Repairs	New display stands	100	
Legal fees	Tax appeal	70	
	Divorce	50	
Depreciation		4,300	
Partners' salaries		7,500	
		£16,575	£120
		120	
Adjusted Schedule D I		£16,455	

Notes:

- As before, wages of wife allowed. Had the wage been excessive, the Revenue may insist on some of it being disallowed.
- The gain on sale is non-trading income and is removed. Other income items are trading income.
- Only private motoring expenses disallowed.
- Only trade subscriptions allowed and only donations which can directly benefit the staff are allowed.
- Entertainment on staff is less than £50 per head – allowed.
- Defalcation (theft) by cashier allowed since he was prosecuted.
- New display stands are capital.
- Tax appeal (Farquarson case) and divorce (personal) disallowed.

Useful references

The following Inland Revenue publications will prove helpful:

IR 64 *Giving to charity – How businesses can get tax relief*
IR 72 *Inland Revenue Investigations – The examination of business accounts*
IR 104 *Tax and your business – Simple tax accounts*

3 Assessment of business profits

What is the assessment based on? □ Assessing commencing businesses □ What happens when the business ceases trading? □ The process for assessing a new business □ Enterprise allowance □ Appendix – Schedule D I assessment on profits

In Chapter 2 we learned the method used by the Revenue to compute the taxable profits of a business. Now that we know how to arrive at the taxable profits for an accounting period, the important questions to ask are:

- how is the profit assessed to income tax?
- when does the tax charged become payable?

Before these questions are answered, it may be helpful to give a brief summary of the time scale involved in issuing assessments and paying the tax. The Inspector of taxes will normally issue assessments for Schedule D I tax between August and October every year, with the tax (and Class 4 NIC – see later) due for payment in two equal instalments, one due on the following 1 January and the other due on 1 July following. Thus the assessments for the tax year 1992/93 will be issued in the autumn of 1992 and the tax is payable on 1 January 1993 and 1 July 1993.

What is the assessment based on?

The normal method of assessing business profits is fairly complicated and readers new to taxation will find it somewhat irrational. In Chapter 2 it was noted, in the list of schedules, that business profits are assessed for a particular tax year on:

the profits of the accounting year ending in the preceding year of assessment

This, it should be stressed, applies only to those businesses which have been running for about three years. For businesses which have just commenced and for those ceasing to trade (or being converted into a company) the system is even more complicated and, at first glance, seems illogical.

Do not panic if, at first, you have difficulty in understanding this concept. You are in good company as almost all students new to taxation find it the most difficult idea of all to grasp.

It is always helpful to use a simple line diagram to illustrate the process:

This is a business which has been in existence for many years, making up accounts at 31 December each year

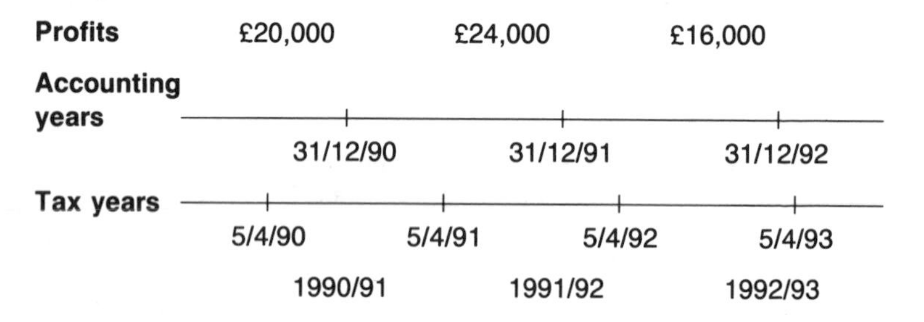

It will be noted that the profit for the year ended 31 December 1991 **ends** in the tax year 1991/92, therefore, it will be assessed to tax for the tax year 1992/93. Taking this the other way round, if you wish to know which profits will be assessed for the tax year 1992/93, we look back to the previous tax year 1991/92 and establish which year of profits **ends** in that tax year. Those will be the profits assessed for 1992/93.

As noted above, the profits earned for the accounting year ended 31 December 1991, £24,000, form the assessment for the tax year 1992/93. This means that the £24,000 becomes the taxable income for all the purposes of taxation (e.g. as a basis for paying pension premiums – see later). The tax (and NIC Class 4 contributions) payable on these profits is due in **two** instalments:

- one half on 1 January 1993
- one half on 1 July 1993.

If we concentrate on the first instalment, it will be noticed that the profits were earned to 31 December 1991 and the tax is not payable until

1 January 1993. This is an interval of **12 months** (and one day!). Yes, it **is** twelve months – although at first glance it may look like **two years**!

A delay in paying tax on profits always arises, the interval between earning the profits and paying the tax depending on the accounting date adopted by the business. This variability can be demonstrated by studying the following table:

Accounts prepared to	*Tax year in which ends*	*Tax year assessed*	*1st instal. due*	*Interval enjoyed*
30/9/91	1991/92	1992/93	1/1/93	15 months
31/3/92	1991/92	1992/93	1/1/93	9 months
30/4/92	1992/93	1993/94	1/1/94	20 months!

In reading the table remember that the profits were always assessed for the tax year **following** that in which the accounting year ends.

If you were given the decision to choose your accounting date, you would of course, opt for a year ending 30 April, giving the maximum cash flow advantage in paying the tax, (if you were really greedy, you would choose 6 April – giving an interval of 21 months!). Many traders, who have taken no advice, have accounting year ends like 23 August or 18 October simply because that particular date happens to be the anniversary of the date they started trading. When you commence trading you can choose **any** accounting date you wish and, clearly, 30 April would have attractions. If you are already in business and now find you have an accounting date which does not give you a significant cash flow advantage, you **can change** the date. Your professional adviser should be consulted as the calculations are reasonably complicated and there may be a compensating disadvantage in terms of the existing assessments being increased (although they can also be reduced given the optimum combination of figures and dates!).

It is most important to appreciate that the above cash flow advantages **only** arise **after** the business has been trading for about **three** years and the intervals indicated do **not** apply in newly formed businesses. Indeed, in new businesses, the position is almost reversed with the tax bills coming thick and fast due to the method of assessing new businesses which will now be discussed.

Assessing commencing businesses

The first point to appreciate is that the normal basis of assessment (i.e. the preceding year basis) simply **cannot** apply in a new business because by its nature **there is no preceding year**. In these circumstances the normal rules of assessment are amended and what follows may surprise you initially. It is not all bad news.

For the purposes of illustrating the rules we will use the following example:

Mr W Payne, a glazier, commenced trading on 1 January 1991 and decides to make up accounts annually at 31 December.

His profits, ignoring capital allowances, as agreed for tax purposes were:

Year ended 31 December 1991	**£ 6,000**
Year ended 31 December 1992	**24,000**
Year ended 31 December 1993	**48,000**

The first important problem to solve is – which tax year do we start counting from? The rule is that the first year of assessment will be the one **during** which the business commenced – in this case 1990/91 (i.e. between 6 April 1990 and 5 April 1991). Notice that the first instalment of that year's tax is due on 1 January 1991! Familiar? Yes it **was** the day the business started. Does this mean that when you open the doors on your first day of trading there is a little brown envelope lying on the mat with the message, 'Welcome to business – here is your tax bill!'. Of course not, because the profits on which to base the assessment will not be known until the accounts for the first year to December 1991 are prepared – sometime early in 1992. However, note carefully that the day **after** 31 December 1991 is 1 January 1992 – the very day the first instalment of the 1991/92 tax is due. Thus, by the time the first set of accounts are submitted **2** tax bills will be due within a short period of time. Hence the warning that, in a new business, tax bills can come thick and fast and the new trader must be alive to this.

We will now look at the method of computing the assessments in the first three years remembering that the normal preceding year basis must be amended.

The first year of assessment, in this case 1990/91, is based on the actual profits earned **during** the tax year in which the business commenced. For this purpose profits are deemed to accrue evenly throughout the accounting year. Thus:

1990/91		
Profits from 1/1/91 to 5/4/91		**Tax due**
3 months = 3/12 × £6,000	£1,500	1/1/91
		1/7/91

(This information is not available till after 31 December 1991 and the tax would be payable 30 days after the issue of the assessment.)

The second year of assessment is, initially, **always** based on the profits earned for the first twelve months of trading so that in this case it becomes:

1991/92		
Profits from 1/1/91 to 31/12/91	£6,000	1/1/92
		1/7/92

(The first instalment of tax would be payable 30 days after the issue of the assessment.)

On being given this information, it must be stated that the average trader's reaction is understandably one of confusion. He says things like 'that is ridiculous' or 'surely there's some mistake'. The trader has, of course, spotted that he has already been taxed on £1,500 of the £6,000 in the first year and he is now being asked to pay tax on the **whole** of the £6,000! Sadly, it gets worse!

The third year of assessment is the first time the preceding year basis can normally be applied. In this case:

1992/93		
Profits for accounting year ending in 1991/92		
i.e. year ending 31/12/91! Again!	£6,000	1/1/93
		1/7/93

This information normally produces total incredulity on the part of the trader and this reaction is understandable. What has happened is that the profit of £6,000 earned for the year to 31 December 1991 has been assessed two and one quarter times! Three months in 1990/91, 12 months in 1991/92 and another 12 months in 1992/93. The reason for this peculiar approach is that a business has to be assessed for all the periods it exists and, since the normal preceding year basis is not available (there being **no** preceding year) the Revenue adopt these rules. A common reaction of traders in this situation is to suggest that they are unhappy about paying tax more than once on the same income and that they would rather pay tax on the 'real income' they earned in each tax year (similar to the calculation for the first year). That would be very bad news for the trader in this example, since this would mean paying tax on the following income:

1991/92

Profits 6/4/91 to 5/4/92	6/4/91–31/12/91 = 9/12 × £ 6,000 =	£ 4,500
	1/1/92–5/4/92 = 3/12 × £24,000 =	6,000
		£10,500

1992/93

Profits 6/4/92 to 5/4/93	6/4/92–31/12/92 = 9/12 × £24,000 =	£18,000
	1/1/93–5/4/93 = 3/12 × £48,000 =	12,000
		£30,000

A quick summary of the figures reveals that, however unfair the system appears to be at first glance, in this case it works to the taxpayer's advantage.

Comparing the two approaches:

	Using Revenue's rules	*Taking actual figures*
1991/92	£ 6,000	£10,500
1992/93	6,000	30,000
Totals	£12,000	£40,500

Which figures would you rather pay tax on?

In this situation it is clearly to the taxypayer's benefit to apply the normal Revenue basis for the first three years bearing in mind that tax will be paid on £6,000 only (less any personal allowances) on 1/1/92 and 1/7/92 (for 1991/92) and on 1/1/93 and 1/7/93 (for

1992/93) during which period profits of £24,000 and £48,000 are being earned. These higher profits will be assessed and taxed on the normal basis as follows:

1993/94 profits for year to 31/12/92	£24,000	Tax due 1/1/94 & 1/7/94
1994/95 profits for year to 31/12/93	£48,000	Tax due 1/1/95 & 1/7/95

An important lesson from all this is that it is no bad thing to have a modest profit for the first year since this gives a breathing space for three years before any major tax bills fall due for payment.

Section 62 election

In the case of the example we have just considered, the rules clearly work in the taxpayer's favour but if this were the full story, then it would be very bad news for a trader whose profits started at a high figure then rapidly diminished. The doubling up of the assessments would then fall on the earlier (and higher) profits and this would be unfair. However, help is at hand in the form of Section 62! This allows the taxpayer to opt to be taxed on the **actual** profits earned during the **second** and **third** tax years instead of under the normal bases.

The following example will illustrate this option.

Mr I Puffin, a tobacconist, started trading on 1 July 1991 and makes up his accounts to 30 June each year. His agreed profits were:

Year ended 30 June 1992	**£40,000**
Year ended 30 June 1993	**12,000**
Year ended 30 June 1994	**16,000**

The assessments would be as follows:

Normal basis	*Section 62 election*	*Final Assessment*
1991/92		
Profits 1/7/91–5/4/92		
9/12 × £40,000 = £30,000		£30,000

1992/93	6/4/92–5/4/93		
Profits of	3/12 × £40,000 = £10,000		
first 12 months £40,000	9/12 × £12,000 = 9,000		
		19,000	£19,000
1993/94			
Preceding year	6/4/93–5/4/94		
profits 30/6/92 £40,000	3/12 × £12,000 = £ 3,000		
	9/12 × £16,000 = 12,000		
		15,000	£15,000

The taxpayer's choice is to take **both** assessments on the normal basis or **both** on an actual basis. Clearly, in this case, the actual basis (Section 62) would be chosen giving total assessments for the years of £34,000 (19,000 + 15,000) compared to £80,000.

Finally, there are some points to bear in mind concerning the election:

- the taxpayer has seven years from the end of the second year of assessment to make the decision – so plenty of time is available.
- the normal assessment for the second year 1992/93 (on £40,000) will be issued once the first year's accounts to 30 June 1992 are submitted, and the tax on £40,000 will be due on the normal dates 1/1/93 and 1/7/93. The information on which the Section 62 figures are calculated for this year (1992/93 – the profits to June 1993 being part of the calculation) will not be available until after 30 June 1993 by which time tax on the £40,000 will have become due. The revised assessment of £19,000 cannot be determined until the second year's results are known and only then can a repayment be made. Similarly the figure of £15,000 for 1993/94 cannot be determined until some time after June 1994. These time scales and the availability and timing of information must be given careful consideration.
- by making an election for Section 62, the doubling of assessments referred to earlier in the chapter do not go away – they simply fall on smaller figures rather than larger figures.

The assessments above would continue:

1994/95	Profits year to 30 June 1993	£12,000
1995/96	Profits year to 30 June 1994	16,000

So that all of the £12,000 would be assessed twice and nine twelfths of the £16,000 would also be assessed twice. Thus, no matter what the dates or amounts are, or whether or not Section 62 is chosen, a doubling of assessment occurs and this can seem unfair.

What happens when the business ceases trading?

The first point to establish is that a cessation, for the purposes of assessment rules can arise as a result of the following events:

- **the permanent cessation of the trade**
- **the admission (or departure) of a partner (see Chapter 5)**
- **the conversion of a sole trader/partnership into a limited company**

The important feature of cessation, for whatever reason, is that quite spectacular savings in tax can be achieved by ceasing at exactly the correct date.

In any cessation there is some good news and some bad news and a later illustration will be used to demonstrate these features and the general rules applying to cessations. Two features will readily become apparent:

- **The anomaly of the double assessment in the early years of a business's life will be compensated for by an amount of profits not being assessed at all. The time period for which profits will not be assessed will exactly equal the time period which was double assessed in a new business. The profits earned in these two periods can, of course, be significantly different.**
- **There are greater planning opportunities present in a ceasing business, the choice of the actual cessation date having important implications for tax mitigation. This involves ensuring that the maximum possible amount of profits drop out of assessment.**

What are the assessment rules?

First it is vitally important to grasp that there **cannot** be an assessment for any tax year **after that in which the business ceased to trade**. For example, if a business ceases trading on 31 December 1992, then the last possible year of assessment is 1992/93.

Thus it is vital to **identify** the last year of assessment and **then** consider the earlier years.

Case study illustration

Mr Noah More has been trading for many years and ceases trading on 31 March 1993.

Agreed profits were:

Year ended 30 April 1989	£12,000
Year ended 30 April 1990	16,800
Year ended 30 April 1991	24,000
Year ended 30 April 1992	36,000
11 months to 31 March 1993	10,000

Good news

Last year becomes:
1992/93 (year of cessation)

The assessment is on the profits earned from 6 April on which the business last traded (6 April 1992) to date of cessation – 31 March 1993.

This produces 1/12 × £36,000 + £10,000 = £13,000
Notice that under the normal preceding year basis that this was originally £24,000
(The taxpayer had received the assessment and paid first instalment of tax on 1/1/93)

This is the only piece of good news in this situation. From here on it is bad news as a result of the rules which apply to the second and third last years.

The basis rules for these years are:

Taken together, the **higher** of the **actual aggregate** profits earned in these years (using time apportionment) or the **original**

assessments for these years on a normal preceding year basis. This is clearly the **Inland Revenue's** choice and is invoked by them under Section 63. This is similar to the taxpayer's choice under Section 62 for the **second** and **third** years of assessment.

Bad news

In this example S. 63 allows the Revenue to revise the second and third last years to the actual basis:

Original		*S. 63*		*Final*
1991/92				
Year ended 30/4/90	£16,800	6/4/91–5/4/92		
		1/12 × £24,000 =	£ 2,000	
		11/12 × 36,000 =	33,000	
			35,000	£35,000
1990/91				
Year ended 30/4/89	£12,000	6/4/90–5/4/91		
		1/12 × £16,800 =	£ 1,400	
		11/12 × 24,000 =	22,000	
			23,400	£23,400
Total for **2** years	£28,800		£58,400	

Thus two assessments, previously agreed and paid – are significantly increased and extra tax is payable forthwith. This is very bad news and there is no appeal. The only comfort is that, in the process certain profits have not been assessed at all.
Amounts not assessed:

Y/E 30 April 1989	£12,000	} 23 months
11/12 × Y/E 30 April 1990	15,400	

Can this situation be rescued or improved? Happily the answer is yes! If we assume that Mr More continued to trade until 30 April 1993 and ceased on that date. In addition, we further assume that his profits for the last month were £900.

The last year is now 1993/94 (year of cessation) and the assessment for that year is 6/4/93–30/4/93 £900

The assessments for the two previous years now become:

	Original	*S. 63*	*Final*
1992/93			
Preceding year 30/4/91	£24,000	6/4/92–5/4/93	
		As above £13,000	£13,000
1991/92			
Preceding year 30/4/90	16,800	As above 35,000	35,000
Total for **2** years	£40,800	£48,000	

Remembering that the **Revenue** will chose the higher **aggregate** figures, then the assessments become £13,000 and £35,000. What is now dropping out of assessment is:

Year ended 30/4/90	£16,800
11/12 x Y/E 30/4/91	22,000

Comparing the assessments arising under the two alternative cessation dates:

	31 March 1993	*30 April 1993*
1992/93	£13,000	£13,000
1991/92	35,000	35,000
1990/91	23,400	12,000
Totals	£71,400	£60,000

Taking these three years, there is a saving in assessments of £11,400 which at 25% = £2,850 and at 40% = £4,560. There is an additional assessment of £900 for 1993/94 on a cessation at 30 April 1993, but even after tax you will still have more cash than if you had ceased at 31 March 1993 and you save tax on £11,400!

Note:
A general rule is that where profits are rising, cease trading AFTER 5 April and if profits are falling, cease trading BEFORE 5 April.

A final comment on cessations

It is most important to keep your professional adviser fully informed of your intentions and to give **reasonable warning** of your intention to take any action which will result in the cessation rules applying. Only then can you be advised of the alternative effects of ceasing at different dates. Having up to date records, which permit accurate estimates of the current and future profits, is of great assistance.

All of this chapter so far assumes that the accounts are drawn up promptly and submitted, with computations, to the Inspector of Taxes shortly afterwards. Sadly, in many cases, this does not happen and the question now arises of the consequences of inaction.

What happens if nothing is done?

Normally the Inland Revenue will become aware of the existence of most new businesses by a variety of means. If a trader registers for VAT or is involved in the PAYE system (for employees) or is in receipt of grants etc., they will come to the attention of the tax district which will be dealing with their affairs. Alternatively, the Revenue will, as a matter of routine, scan local papers where traders may be advertising their services. If a company is formed, the Revenue will quickly pick this up. When the Revenue does become aware of the business, a Form 41G will be sent to it requesting information concerning the business and its owners; the accounting date; and the name of any agent acting for the business. If for some reason the Revenue fail to get in touch with a business, the owners should inform them that a business has been started. Failure to do so could create serious problems at a later date – such as three or more assessments becoming due at the same time with the possibility of interest and penalties being added! It is not worth the risk!

The process for assessing a new business

If, after about three months following the end of the first year's trading, accounts have not been submitted to the Inspector of Taxes, he will issue **estimated** assessments, usually for the first two years of assessment. The tax for the first year being due within thirty days of the date of the assessment and tax for the second year being due at dates dependent on when the accounting date is (some of this could also be due within thirty days). The estimated figures are based on the Inspector's experience of similar businesses and great care should be taken when such assessments are received. They **cannot** be ignored! If the trader feels that the figures are excessive, an appeal must be made by the taxpayer, or an agent acting on a mandate, within **thirty** days of the date on the assessment. An inspector has discretion to accept late appeals, but good reasons must accompany such a request. The appeal must give precise reasons why the figures are excessive e.g. the profits shown by the business's accounts are lower than the assessment; capital allowances will be claimed which do not appear on the assessment or perhaps the assessment does not grant full allowances (check that the annual income tax return has been submitted!). A most important feature of the appeal is that it **must** indicate how much tax (and NIC) the taxpayer feels *should* be payable and request that the excessive tax be **postponed**.

Failure to ask for such postponement will result in ALL the tax (and NIC) shown on the assessment becoming payable on the dates shown. It is most important to bring any assessments received to the attention of an adviser. If a mandate has been completed in favour of an adviser at an earlier date then the adviser should receive copies of all such assessments.

Enterprise allowance

As an incentive for individuals to become self employed (the enterprise culture at work!), the government will pay individuals who satisfy certain conditions, a sum of £40 per week for the first year of their new business. This is subject to tax and NIC in the same way as other income. However, given that this is paid in the first year, the assessment rules would result in this allowance being taxed more than once! This was not intended and, after the scheme had been running for a short time, special rules were introduced to prevent the double assessment. The amount of the enterprise allowance is shown separately in the accounts and not included in the overall profit figure. The opening years' assessments are then computed on the profit excluding the allowance which is assessed, under Schedule D VI, on the amounts actually received in each tax year.

Appendix – Schedule D I assessment on profits

There is shown below a typical Schedule D I assessment on profits.

Year Ended 5 April 1993
Mr B Dover
Notice of Assessment

		Ref No	
	£	£	
Fishmonger		28,000	
Trading deductions:			
Capital allowances		2,400	
Total chargeable		25,600	
Allowances:			
Pension payments	3,000		
Class 4 NIC relief	471		
Personal allowance	3,445		
Married couple's allowance	1,720		
Total		8,636	
Net Chargeable to Tax		16,964	
Tax Chargeable:			
First £2,000 at 20%		400	
Basic rate at 25% on £14,964		3,741	(A)
Class 4 National Insurance		4,141	
Profit (less Capital allowances)		25,600	
Lower Limit		6,120	
Charged at 6.3% on	(maximum)	14,940	
Payable		941.22	(B)
Total payable	A + B	5,082.22	

Due: 1/1/93 – ½ £2,541.11. 1/7/93 – ½ £2,541.11

Note:

The capital allowances referred to above are dealt with fully in Chapter 4 and the various rates of National Insurance Contributions are shown in an Appendix at the end of Chapter 9. A Schedule D I taxpayer is allowed a deduction in his personal computation equal to 50% of the amount of Class 4 NIC paid by him on his profits.

The basis of assessment – proposed reforms

During 1991, the Inland Revenue issued a consultative paper proposing simplified rules for assessing income under Schedule D cases I and II. If implemented, these proposals will sweep away most of the present complexities and anomalies (and opportunities!). However, implementation of these rules is some years off.

Useful references

The following Inland Revenue publications will prove helpful:

IR 26 *Income Tax assessments on business profits – Changes of accounting date*
IR 28 *Tax and your business – Starting in business*
IR 37 *Income Tax and Capital Gains Tax – Appeals*
IR 57 *Thinking of working for yourself?*
IR 105 *Tax and your business – How your profits are taxed*

4 Capital allowances

Plant and machinery □ Industrial buildings allowances (IBA) □ Agricultural buildings allowances (ABA) □ Other items subject to allowances

In Chapter 2 it was noted that any expenditure on capital items – land and buildings, plant and machinery, equipment and motor vehicles – was disallowed in arriving at the taxable profit of the business. In other words, the taxable profit is not simply the difference between cash received and cash spent. It is the difference between the income generated in an accounting period (whether or not the cash is collected in that period) and the allowable **Revenue** expenditure incurred in the period (whether or not the expenses were paid in the period). A much fuller coverage of this area is provided by Geoffrey Whitehead in *Book-keeping & Accounting* in the NatWest Series.

It was also noted that any amount charged in the Profit and Loss Account in respect of depreciation was also disallowed. This approach is based on the principle that depreciation is simply a method of writing off capital expenditure over the life of an asset rather than writing off the whole cost in the year in which the expenditure was incurred.

Thus at this stage it seems that no allowance has been made for capital expenditure and, as far as adjusting the Profit and Loss Account is concerned, that is exactly the position.

However, help is at hand! It is called the capital allowances system. This is a system under which a standard rate of allowance is granted in respect of certain types of capital expenditure. It is most important at this stage to appreciate that, simply because an item of expenditure is classified as capital and therefore disallowed in arriving at the taxable profit, it will not automatically qualify for capital allowances. The worst scenario is that an item is disallowed **AND** fails to qualify for capital allowances. Ask the owners of Wimpy and Pizzaland! (see later).

The capital allowances system deals separately with different types of expenditure, with different rules both in terms of identifying which items qualify for allowances and in terms of the rates of allowances available. The legislation is contained in the Capital Allowances Act 1990. The areas on which this book concentrates are those most commonly encountered by small businesses:

- **Plant and machinery**
- **Industrial buildings**
- **Enterprise Zone buildings**
- **Agricultural land and buildings**
- **Patents**

Capital allowances may also be claimed on the following items of expenditure:

- Mines and oil wells
- Dredging
- Scientific research
- Acquisition of know how
- Cemeteries and crematoria.

As it is unlikely that these affect many small businesses, only brief reference will be made to them.

Plant and machinery

Almost every small business will be able to claim some capital allowances under this heading and it is important to appreciate what the term includes. Plant and machinery, for capital allowances purposes includes all moveable and fixed items of equipment including:

- desks and chairs
- computers
- moveable partitions
- fork lift trucks
- lorries
- central heating
- motor cars (special rules apply)

A helpful definition was given in the case *Yarmouth* v. *France*, 1887 where the judge defined plant as being 'all apparatus, live or dead, used by a businessman in carrying on his trade'. Even horses are included! The important words are '**in carrying on his trade**'.

The following are examples of items which the courts have decided do **not** qualify for capital allowances:

- Display or background lighting in a retail store – *Cole Bros* v. *Philips*, 1982 – regarded as the 'setting' in which the business was conducted rather than something used in carrying on the trade.
- The canopy of a petrol station was also regarded as 'setting' and did not qualify – *Dixon* v. *Fitch Garages Ltd*, 1975.
- Floor and wall tiles and decor, shop front – *Wimpy International and Pizzaland* v. *Warland*, 1989 – again regarded as setting and part of the fabric of the building. Perversely, the lighting *was* allowed as it was regarded as necessary to create the required 'ambience' for the fast food business.

The following are examples of expenditure which **did** qualify as Plant for capital allowances purposes:

- Moveable office partitions – *Jarrold* v. *John Good and Sons Ltd*, 1963.
- Background lighting and decor in hotels and bars – *Scottish and Newcastle Breweries*, 1982. The judge took the view that such lighting was necessary to create the correct 'ambience' in which customers could relax and enjoy their pint! It does contrast markedly with the *Cole Bros* case above.

The following expenditure also attracts capital allowances under the arrangements for Plant:

- Fire safety
- Heat insulation of industrial buildings
- Safety expenditure in sports stadia
- Security assets to protect individuals

These examples serve as a general guide and, before embarking on substantial capital expenditure, advice should be sought on whether capital allowances will be available. An alternative to buying an item of equipment on which capital allowances may not be available would be to lease it. Apart from the obvious cash flow advantages – not having to pay the full price now – the annual leasing charge will normally be deducted in full in arriving at the taxable profit. Leasing, of course, is always an alternative to buying outright and many leasing arrangements permit the lessor to take over the asset at the end of the lease at a favourable price. If items are bought on hire purchase, then **full** capital allowances may be claimed on the **cash** price only. The interest paid during the year is deducted in arriving at the trading profit.

Rates of allowances:

For all items classified as Plant (other than motor cars costing over £12,000).	A writing down allowance (WDA) of 25% p.a. is given on the reducing balance method.
Cars costing over £12,000 (£8,000 for cars bought pre 11/3/92).	25% WDA (maximum £3,000 per car per annum).

The above rates are the maximum amounts which may be claimed and a taxpayer may choose to claim either a smaller amount or indeed no allowances at all in any particular year, with the unclaimed cost being carried forward to be claimed in future years. This may be advantageous where the present income is small and is extinguished by personal allowances and in later years higher rate tax may be payable.

Allowances are given on the capital expenditure incurred less any part of the cost met by another person (including the Department of Trade and Industry). Note, however, that any grants received under the Industry Act 1972 (Regional Development Grants) are not deducted from the cost and capital allowances are given on the **full** cost.

When are allowances given?

To understand the answer to this question it is necessary to refer back to the rules of assessment for unincorporated businesses covered in Chapter 3.

The allowances will be first claimable for the **tax** year, in the basis period for which, the expenditure is incurred. Thus if a taxpayer makes up accounts to 31 December each year, then any expenditure during the year ended 31 December 1992 will first qualify for capital allowances for the tax year 1993/94 and be set against the profit for the year to 31 December 1992.

It becomes important, therefore, for a business approaching the end of its accounting year to consider what might be spent on assets. To delay the expenditure into the next accounting year will delay the benefit of any capital allowances for a full year. Obviously, a close control over the cash position of the business will permit such decisions to be taken with confidence. This is particularly true in the first tax year of a new business, where the cut-off date for determining which year benefits from capital allowances is 5 April, regardless of the accounting date.

How are the allowances computed?

For the purposes of computing capital allowances for plant, the assets are dealt with in 'pools' of expenditure. Most businesses will operate two pools:

- one containing all qualifying assets other than private cars
- one containing all private cars costing less than £12,000 each.

Any private cars costing over £12,000 and any assets with any private (non-business) use are treated as individual items. The advantage of the pooling system is that any individual gains arising on the sale of an individual asset contained in a pool are ignored for tax purposes. However, any losses are similarly ignored. Clearly where an item is treated individually, then gains and losses do arise. These are called, respectively, balancing charges (taxable gains) and balancing allowances (allowable losses).

There are certain assets which will almost certainly result in a loss when sold, mainly high tech items such as computers. To allow such a loss to emerge, such items (known as 'short-life assets') may be 'de-pooled' and treated on an individual basis.

Where there has been agreement with the Inspector of Taxes that a proportion of an asset's use is private (usually motor cars), then the available capital allowance is restricted to the business use proportion only.

The following example illustrates the above points:

Mr Pat McAuley, a dog trainer, has been in business for many years and makes up accounts to 30 September each year. During the year to

30 September 1991 he sold a trailer for £1,200 and a car (original cost £5,000) for £2,600. He purchased a second-hand lorry for £6,000 and a heating unit for £1,400.

The balances brought forward at 6 April 1992 were:

	General pool	*Cars under £8,000 (3)*	*Car over £8,000 – private use 50% (bought pre 11/3/92)*	*Total allowances*
	£	£	£	
	14,000	12,000	16,000	
1992/93				
Sold	1,200	2,600		
	12,800	9,400		
Bought	6,000			
	1,400			
	20,200	9,400	16,000	
WDA 25%	5,050	2,350	Max. 2,000 × 50%	£8,400
C/Fwd	15,150	7,050	14,000	

Mr McAuley may deduct capital allowances of £8,400 from his Schedule D I profits assessed for 1992/93.

Note that the allowance on the expensive car is restricted to £2,000 and further restricted to 50% for private use.

Had Mr McAuley sold all the private cars in the year to September 1991 for say £9,000, a balance of £3,000 would remain on which WDA could be claimed. Had he sold them for £13,000, a balancing charge, representing taxable income, of £1,000 would arise and there would be no balance left to carry forward.

The balances brought forward at 6 April 1992 represent the original costs of the assets less any capital allowances claimed up to 1991/92.

Industrial buildings allowances (IBA)

Industrial buildings allowances are unlikely to have a major impact on most small businesses (unless the building is situated in an Enterprise Zone – see below) since the rate of allowance is extremely modest.

What is an industrial building

The question of whether IBA may be claimed in respect of expenditure on a building has little to do with the nature of the structure. It has everything to do with the trade (or activity) which is carried on in the building. The following activities **qualify**:

- manufacturing or processing of goods
- businesses concerned with water, electricity, hydraulic power, tunnels, mines and bridges
- buildings to store goods used by or produced by a manufacturing or processing business
- maintenance or repair of goods or materials (provided business is not part of a retail business). This is the activity in which many small businesses are engaged.

Buildings on which **no** IBA is available include retail shops, showrooms and offices (but see below).

What expenditure qualifies?

Provided a qualifying trade is being carried on, then expenditure on a **new** building qualifies for an annual IBA (currently 4 per cent based on cost price). The cost of land never qualifies but the costs of preparing the land for building do. Drawing offices and canteens qualify provided they form part of the industrial complex. Administration offices qualify, provided they are part of the building and their cost does not exceed 25 per cent of the total qualifying expenditure. Curiously, sports pavilions provided for the welfare of staff in **any** trade qualify.

Expenditure on hotels qualifies for IBA provided certain conditions are satisfied – they are open at least four months between April and October with a minimum of ten letting rooms.

So far the allowances appear to be very modest at 4 per cent of cost. However, there are two situations where the allowances available are extremely attractive.

1. Buildings constructed in Enterprise Zones

These are specially designated areas in various parts of the UK, where the Government, in an attempt to attract employers, offers a series of inducements. The most useful one is that an IBA of 100 per cent is given to the purchaser of a new building in such an area. This allowance is available on **most** buildings (except dwelling houses), regardless of the trade being conducted. Even where a second-hand building, originally constructed in the zone, is acquired, substantial allowances may be available.

2. Second-hand industrial buildings

The tax life of an industrial building is 25 years (for buildings constructed post 6 November 1962 – for older buildings the tax life is 50 years). This means that if a building over 25 years old is purchased then **no** allowances can be claimed by the purchaser. Also no balancing charge can arise on the seller!

When a second-hand building is purchased, the purchaser will not be given IBA in the usual way (4 per cent p.a.). Instead, he will be given total allowances of the **lower** of:

- the price paid for the building

OR

- its original cost to the first owner

spread evenly over the building's remaining tax life at the date of purchase.

Example

Mr A buys a building from Mr B for £40,000 in January 1992. Mr B had bought the building new in January 1969 for £25,000. Both were in qualifying trades.

Mr A will get allowances of £25,000 spread over the two years 1992 and 1993 i.e. £12,500 p.a. Note that he does **not** get allowances on £40,000!

Consider what would have happened had the building been:

- 26 years old — **no** allowances available
- 3 years old — allowances would be spread over 22 years giving a small allowance each year (the price would obviously be different)

The moral is – before buying a building, find out its age and original cost! While an older building may be attractive from a tax point of view, commercial realism must prevail in making the decision.

The older building may be more expensive to maintain – higher repair and insurance bills, more expensive to heat. In addition it may be more difficult to raise finance or obtain grants in respect of older buildings. The situation can be complicated if the building has not qualified throughout its life. This is outside the scope of this book.

Agricultural buildings allowances (ABA)

This allowance, at the rate of 4 per cent p.a., is given on the cost incurred by an owner or tenant of agricultural land when he or she incurs expenditure on a farmhouse, farm buildings, cottages, fences or other works. It should be noted that only one third of the cost of any farmhouse can qualify for ABA.

4

On a sale of such items, provided the original expenditure was not incurred prior to 1 April 1986, the new and old owners can jointly elect for a balancing adjustment (balancing charge or allowance) to arise. The new owner is given allowances in the same way as those applying to second-hand industrial buildings (see above).

If no election is made, the new owner simply takes over the annual allowances (at 4 per cent p.a.) from the date of sale till the building is 25 years old. The whole interest in the land must be transferred to allow this procedure to apply. An owner may not grant a leasehold to an incoming tenant.

Other items subject to allowances

There now follows a brief summary of the allowances available on some other items mentioned at the start of this chapter.

Patents

Where patent rights are purchased, a WDA of 25 per cent p.a. on a reducing balance method is given. Expenditure is pooled.

Scientific research

An allowance is given of 100 per cent of expenditure incurred by a trader. Expenditure on land is excluded.

Know-how

This means expenditure on industrial information (legally obtained!) and techniques. The allowance is 25 per cent on a reducing balance method.

Useful references

The following Inland Revenue publications will prove helpful:

IR 106 *Tax and your business – Capital allowances for vehicles and machinery*

CA1 *Income Tax and Corporation Tax – Capital allowances for machinery or plant.* (Plus supplement)

CA2 *Income Tax and Corporation Tax – Capital allowances on industrial buildings.* (Plus supplement)

CA4 *Income Tax and Corporation Tax – Allowances for scientific research*

5 Partnerships

What is a partnership for tax purposes? □ How are partners taxed? □ How are the profits for tax purposes computed? □ What happens if there is a change of partners? □ Can the partnership rules be used to minimise tax? □ Are there any tax pitfalls?

So far, this book has focused exclusively on the taxation of sole traders. In this section the taxation treatment of a very common form of business structure, partnerships, will be considered.

Fortunately, there are very few new rules to learn, since all of the assessment rules applicable to sole traders apply to partnerships. The method of assessing ongoing, commencing and ceasing businesses apply, and indeed, in a partnership, the commencement and cessation rules have a very special role to play in the tax planning areas relevant to partnerships. There is one very important addition to the general rules, and this can arise where there is a change in the personnel of the partnership. This will be discussed later in this chapter.

First, there are a few fundamental questions which must be asked.

What is a partnership for tax purposes?

The legal definition of a partnership is given in the Partnership Act of 1890 as '*the relationship which subsists between persons carrying on a business in common with a view of profit*'.

Whether a partnership exists for tax purposes is a question of fact. It is not sufficient simply to have an agreement which states that a partnership exists; the actions of the parties involved must clearly indicate that they are 'carrying on a business with a view of profit'. Any agreement amongst partners may and **should** be in writing, but the absence of such a document does not indicate that no partnership exists. The agreement can be an oral one but this is not a clever idea.

How are partners taxed?

It is important to understand that the assessments to tax are not made on individual partners but **jointly on the partnership** and, since partners are 'jointly and severally' liable for the debts of the partnership, any one partner could – if the others are insolvent – be held liable for the **whole** of the tax bill!

The total tax due by a partnership is arrived at by the following steps:

---

1. **The profits assessed for the tax year (on a normal preceding year basis) are allocated amongst the partners according to their agreement – see below.**
2. **The tax bill for each partner is then calculated individually taking into account their personal circumstances e.g. married or single, mortgage relief, etc.**
3. **The individual tax bills of all the partners are then aggregated and the total becomes a partnership liability, with the joint and several rule applying.**
4. **There are a number of ways of settling the liability. Each partner could pay in the amount of their individual liability and the partnership would pay the full amount to the Revenue. Alternatively, if there were enough funds in its bank, the partnership could pay the full amount, with the individual partners' current accounts being charged with each one's share.**

How does the Partnership Agreement affect the tax position?

The contents of the agreement will determine the way in which the profits of the firm are allocated for tax purposes. It should make reference to:

- **the method of sharing profits and losses**
- **the amount of salary to be paid to any particular partner. This salary would represent the differing contributions made in terms of time and effort by each partner. One may work full time and another part time**
- **the amount of any interest on capital to be paid (or credited) to each partner. This would reflect the differing capital contributed by each partner**

- **the procedures to be followed when an existing partner leaves (or dies) or a new partner is admitted. In this section of the agreement there must be very specific clauses relating to taxation matters. It is vital that such clauses are included as will become apparent later.**

While the above sections of an agreement have particular relevance to the taxing of the partnership, there are other, non-tax areas which must be included such as:

- the arrangements for partners drawings, specifying agreed limits
- any rules concerning the behaviour and duties of each partner, e.g. cheque signatories
- the procedure on dissolution of the partnership.

How are the profits for tax purposes computed?

The rules for computing taxable profits are exactly those described in Chapter 2 with one important addition. Any salaries taken by partners and any interest on their capitals are regarded as appropriations of profits and not charges against the profits and are **never** allowed in computing the taxable profits.

How are the profits allocated?

This is done in three stages:

---

1. **Any salaries and interest on capital (as enjoyed during the tax year concerned) are first allocated to each partner**
2. **The balance of profits are then allocated to the partners in the profit sharing ratios as enjoyed during the tax year concerned.**
3. **Finally, the salary, interest on capital and the share of profits above are added together to arrive at each partner's share of the firm's total taxable profits for the year.**

Note that the salaries, interest and profit sharing ratios used are those enjoyed during the tax year being assessed and **not** those during the basis period in which the profits were earned.

This process is best illustrated by a worked example. For simplicity, no interest on capital has been included.

Messrs Green, White and Gold have been trading in partnership for many years under the following arrangements:

	Share of profits	*Salaries p.a. (fixed)*
Green	1/2	£2,400
White	1/3	4,000
Gold	1/6	8,000

The adjusted profits for tax purposes i.e. before charging any salaries, for the year ended 31 March 1992 was agreed at £32,400.

The allocation of the assessment for 1992/93 (preceding year basis):

	Salary	*Share of balance*	*Total*
Green	£ 2,400	£ 9,000	£11,400
White	4,000	6,000	10,000
Gold	8,000	3,000	11,000
Totals	£14,400	£18,000	£32,400

The order in which the above table has been completed is important and the steps are as follows:

1 Enter the final assessment – £32,400 – in the bottom right hand corner (this must be the amount finally allocated).
2 Enter the figures for the annual salaries and add them.
3 Establish the balance to be allocated in the profit sharing ratio (£32,400 less £14,400).
4 Allocate the £18,000 in the appropriate ratios.
5 Add the salary and share figures for each partner and enter in total column, checking it adds to £32,400.

Each of the individual tax bills will be computed by reference to the figures in the right hand column, the aggregate of these becoming the partnership tax liability.

Had the salaries not been fixed and had been changed with effect from 1 April 1992 to:

Green	£ 6,000
White	2,400
Gold	12,000

Then the allocation would be:

	Salary	*Share of balance*	*Total*
Green	£ 6,000	£ 6,000	£12,000
White	2,400	4,000	6,400
Gold	12,000	2,000	14,000
Totals	£20,400	£12,000	£32,400

This produces the rather strange situation where the figures used for accounting purposes during the basis period for 1992/93 (year to 31 March 1992) are different from those used to compute the respective tax liabilities of the individual partners. The rationale underlying this approach is that profits are assessed on a *preceding* basis but salaries are assessed on an *actual* tax year basis.

What happens if there is a change of partners?

This is the major area in partnership taxation and an understanding of the processes involved depends on an appreciation of the rules for assessing new and ceasing businesses covered in Chapter 3.

The first point to note is that where any change takes place in the composition of the members of a partnership, then under Section 113 (1), one business is deemed to cease and a new business deemed to start. This happens despite the fact that the business is continuing exactly as before, in the same trade and with the same set of records, etc. This would bring into play all the rules of assessment covering ceasing businesses and, as we will see, a modified version of the commencement rules. The application of the ceasing rules, can, as we have seen, result in greatly increased assessments for the second and third last years of assessment by virtue of the Revenue's right to invoke Section 63, revising these years to an actual basis. This would be most unfair to those partners who were continuing in the firm and who were not ceasing to trade.

What can the partners do about this?

Fortunately, under Section 113 (2), where there is at least one partner common to the old and the new business, then an election, signed by **all** partners in the old and the new firms within two years of any change, allows the firm to be assessed on a normal continuation basis, using the preceding year approach.

This removes the possibility of Section 63 being applied and means that the rules for new businesses are ignored. The application of this continuation basis does however produce some anomalous situations, especially where one partner is joining as another is leaving. This will be illustrated shortly.

Clearly this election would be made in situations where the profits leading up to the date of the change were increasing, since in this situation, the actual profits for the second and third last tax years would be higher than the figures using the preceding year basis (which would be earlier and, therefore, smaller profits) and the Revenue would obviously invoke Section 63.

The mechanics of a Section 113 election for continuation are as follows:

- **The tax year during which the change took place is identified.**
- **The profits assessed for this tax year are established using the normal preceding year basis.**
- **These profits are then apportioned to the two firms involved by reference to how long each firm existed during this tax year.**

This means that the allocation of the profits amongst the partners must be done in two parts, one for each part of the tax year involved.

The following simple illustration will make the process clear:

Messrs A, B and C have been trading in partnership for many years, making up accounts to 31 December each year. Profits are shared equally and there were no salaries paid. Mr C leaves on 30 June 1992 and A and B continue trading in partnership, sharing profits equally. Profits, agreed for tax were:

Year ended 31 December 1990	£60,000
Year ended 31 December 1991	72,000
Year ended 31 December 1992	84,000

Since profits are rising, the firm would not wish a cessation to take place at 30 June 1992. A continuation election would be signed by A, B and C before 30 June 1994. The result would be:

- Tax year of change? 1992/93
- Assessed for 1992/93? Year ended 31 December 1991 – £72,000
- Split 1992/93 tax year at 30 June 1992:
  6/4/92–30/6/92 = 3 months as firm A, B & C – 3/12 = £18,000
  1/7/92–5/4/93 = 9 months as firm A & B – 9/12 = £54,000

Allocation of 1992/93 assessments:

		A	*B*	*C*
3 months to 30/6/92	£18,000	£ 6,000	£ 6,000	£ 6,000
9 months to 5/4/93	54,000	27,000	27,000	–
Total assessed	72,000	33,000	33,000	6,000

Notice that the last profits on which Mr C was assessed were three months out of the twelve months to 31 December 1991. He was not assessed on **nine** months of this profit, nor was he assessed on any of the six months up to 30 June 1992, the date he left. But this is not a surprise since as we saw, when someone ceases trading, certain profits drop out! Mr C **is** ceasing to trade and therefore, as far as **he** is concerned profits **do** drop out.

Admitting a new partner

The situation becomes just a little more complicated when a new partner is admitted. This situation often coincides with a partner leaving – one usually buying the share of the other.

If we assume, returning to the above example, that Mr D joined the firm at the time C left and that Mr D has an equal share of profits, we will see that it is sometimes difficult to explain the outcome to D.

The assessment for the tax year 1992/93 would now be split between two firms as follows:

A, B & C 3 months to 30/6/92 – 3/12 × £72,000 = £18,000
A, B & D 9 months to 5/4/93 – 9/12 × £72,000 = £54,000

These figures would be allocated (1992/93):

		A	*B*	*C*	*D*
Firm A B & C	£18,000	£ 6,000	£ 6,000	£ 6,000	
Firm A B & D	54,000	18,000	18,000	–	£18,000
Totals	72,000	24,000	24,000	6,000	18,000

Mr D will probably express some surprise at the fact that he is paying tax on income which he had no part in earning and did not receive! He is being asked to pay tax on his share of nine months of the profits for the year ended 31 December 1991 and he did not become a partner till 30 June 1992! There is worse news. He will also pay tax on his share of six months profits of the year to 31 December 1992 which he did not earn or enjoy. However, he must pay tax on some figure for each tax year he is in business and in this case he is much better off paying tax for 1992/93 and 1993/94 on a share of £72,000, rather than on a share of £84,000. If a cessation had taken place, ½ × £84,000 would have entered into 1992/93 and 1993/94 assessments.

In this example electing for Section 113 was better for all the parties involved. This may not always be the case and, bearing in mind that the election must be unanimous, there could be problems if one partner refuses to sign. It is wise, therefore, for the partnership agreement to contain a clause requiring an incoming or outgoing partner to sign a Section 113 election if required to do so by the continuing partners.

What happens if no election is made for the continuance basis?

As indicated above, the cessation of one firm is deemed to have taken place and another to have started. The fact that this happened was, up until 1985, the subject of an extraordinary level of abuse by large partnerships, resulting in huge reductions in their tax bills. Briefly, what these firms would do was as follows:

- Cause a technical cessation by having a partner join or leave (often someone whose only role was to create the cessation)
- The cessation would be timed when the profits had reached the highest point and levelled out. In this way, Section 63 would not be invoked and large profits would drop out of assessment.

- The firm would then endeavour to have the first year of the 'new' firm showing very modest profits – maybe the principals had a long holiday spending the profits which had escaped tax! This modest profit, under the commencement rules, would form the assessment for the next **three** years as described in Chapter 3. After the 'poor' year the firm would, of course, start to make huge profits again!

This operation could be, and **was**, carried out by some firms every five years.

This jolly wheeze was severely curtailed by provisions contained in the 1985 Finance Act, now incorporated in the ICTA 1988.

The position now is that where a change takes place and the firm **could** have elected for the continuance basis but chose **not** to do so, then the year of the change **and the following three years** must **all** be based on the actual profits for each of those tax years. Thus the ruse of having one 'poor' year no longer works.

The election to have the second and third years of assessment based on the actual results (Section 62 as described in Chapter 3) cannot apply. However, there is a similar election available to a firm to which these modified rules apply. This election applies to years FIVE and SIX. These modified rules for assessing firms **do not apply** to the following situations:

- Where a sole trader takes on a partner or partners
- Where members of a partnership leave the firm to be run by one partner as a sole trader.

In these cases the normal cessation and commencement rules apply if no election is made for continuance and this can produce the advantages of profits dropping out and the first three years of the 'new' business being based on the first year's profits. However, in such changes, an election for continuance **can** be made if desired.

Can the partnership rules be used to minimise tax?

There are at least three ways in which the rules and elections might work to the taxpayer's advantage.

- Where a sole trader converts to a partnership (or vice versa) the original pre-1985 plan can still work – profits dropping out and three years based on a low profit (as above).

- Where two persons are considering going into business in partnership, it may be worth considering whether one of them should be an **employee** of the firm for the first year of trading and, at the end of the first year, be assumed as a partner with a continuance election being made. The employee would pay tax and NIC once (under the PAYE arrangements) but the wage paid plus the employer's NIC would be a deduction in arriving at the first year's profits (perhaps halving them?).

  These much reduced profits would then form the basis for the first **three** years' assessments, two of which would be split equally between two partners!
- Where a sole trader is making modest profits and is considering selling the business to someone who can make it very profitable, there may be scope for making the existing owner a partner, signing an election under Section 113, and being taxed on a share of the modest profits instead of the actual profits which might be much higher. The original owner can then leave, signing another Section 113 election! You can have as many of these as you wish. This latter idea would work only in limited circumstances.
- A wife can be a most useful partner – from a business point of view! If a businessman is running a successful business and has had a spectacularly good year, say profits for year ended 31 December 1991 were £100,000 (assessed for 1992/93). If he can justify his wife becoming a partner – she already works full time in the business in a senior position or is skilled in the work of the business – then huge tax savings can be made. If she is made an equal partner on 6 April 1992 and the assessment for 1992/93 (£100,000) is shared equally between them, the result is significant savings at the higher rate of tax – 40 per cent!

  It would be difficult to use this approach in certain businesses like professional firms such as solicitors, accountants or architects where special qualifications may be required and are not necessarily held by both spouses.

Are there any tax pitfalls?

Before discussing the specific taxation aspects, the most recurring problems in partnerships are to do with the fact that the partners simply fall out! The problems are often exacerbated as a result of there being no formal written partnership agreement. It is, therefore, most important, before entering into a partnership:

- To have some prior knowledge of your partners both on a personal level and from a financial point of view. Preferably, you should have worked with them.
- To have a very comprehensive partnership agreement drawn up by a solicitor. If individual partners have their own solicitors, then the proposed agreement should be shown to them. Ensure that the agreement is 'tailored' to the requirements of the business and not simply a standard pro forma agreement lifted off the shelf. Finally, **ensure that an accountant has scrutinised it** and satisfied himself regarding the inclusion of any tax clauses.
- To realise that you are entering into an arrangement where your **liability is unlimited** and that you can be held liable for the other partners' share of any business debts.

The tax problems which can arise are as follows:

- As indicated earlier, you **may** become responsible for the tax liabilities of other partners.
- Unless there are clear provisions regarding the procedures on a change of partners (Section 113 (2) election for continuance), then a difficult partner who refuses to sign the election can create unnecessary additional liabilities for the other partners.
- Finally, the most worrying possibility of all. This concerns a partner who has recently left a firm and who, at the date of his departure, signed an election for continuance under Section 113 (2).

  This was done because all the partners involved agreed that, given the trend of profits at that time, this was the most tax efficient course of action. However, if within two years of this change there is a permanent discontinuance of the trade, or another change in partners resulting in a cessation arising (no continuance election), then the partner who left could suddenly find himself saddled with an additional assessment as a result of an event over which he had no control or a decision in which he played no part.

This problem can be illustrated by the following example:

Bell, Book and Connell have been trading in partnership for many years, sharing profits and losses as follows:
Bell – 2/5, Book – 2/5, Connell – 1/5. No salaries were paid. Mr Bell retired on 5 July 1990, the other two continuing the business sharing profits equally. A continuation election was signed.

The business makes up accounts each year to 31 March, recent profits being:

31 March 1990	£10,000
31 March 1991	60,000
31 March 1992	12,000
31 March 1993	48,000

On 5 July 1992 Mr Brown was admitted as an equal partner with Book and Connell. No continuance election was signed.
The solution will focus on the effect of these events on Mr Bell.

Mr Bell's retirement

Tax year of change? – 1990/91.
Assessment? £10,000 (year ended 31 March 1990).

Allocation: Bell, Book and Connell 6/4/90–5/7/90 = 1/4 – £2,500
Mr Bell's share – 2/5 = £1,000

Mr Brown's admission – cessation at 5 July 1992

Last year of assessment becomes 1992/93, the Revenue can invoke Section 63 for 1990/91 and 1991/92.

	Normal basis *Preceding year*	*Section 63* *Actual basis*
1990/91	£10,000	£60,000
1991/92	60,000	12,000
Totals	70,000	72,000

The Revenue will invoke Section 63 with disastrous results for Mr Bell since 1990/91 is now assessed on £60,000 instead of £10,000! The partnership of Bell, Book and Connell will be assessed for 1990/91 on 1/4 of £60,000 = £15,000, with Mr Bell's share of 2/5 being £6,000! When he left the firm he was assessed on £1,000 for 1990/91 and this now becomes £6,000. Imagine another zero on these numbers!

Can anything be done?

The answer is sometimes. There must be a clause in the partnership agreement indemnifying any outgoing partner against any additional tax liability falling upon that partner as a result of events taking place after he left the firm. In other words, the other partners will pay the additional tax arising. However, such a clause will have no authority where all of the existing partners are insolvent, and the provisions of partnership law will apply, making Mr Bell not only liable for his own extra tax for the three months of 1990/91 but for that of the other partners as well! It can be most unfair.

---

6 Trading losses

How are trading losses computed? □ Section 380 □ Carry forward loss under Section 385 □ Losses in new businesses – Section 381 □ Terminal losses – Section 388 □ Transfer of a business to a limited company – Section 386 □ The role of capital allowances in loss claims – Section 383

In all of the previous chapters it has been assumed that every business always makes a profit. As those in business are all too aware, losses are occasionally made. This chapter will deal with the taxation implications of making a trading loss. It is entirely logical that if trading profits are charged to tax, then trading losses (or negative profits?) should be the subject of some form of relief from tax. It can be an extremely complicated area, especially where losses are sustained in the early years of a business, and in a book of this type it is sufficient that the reader is made aware of the operation of the main methods of relief available.

How are trading losses computed?

Losses are computed in **exactly** the same manner as that used in computing taxable trading profits. All of the rules described in Chapter 2 apply and an allowable trading loss is the product of applying the methods shown in that chapter. The only additional step is to **add** to whatever trading loss the process produces, any capital allowances available for the same period as that for which the loss was computed. This is optional (see later).

How is the loss relieved?

Trading losses can be relieved against:

- current income
- future income
- past income
- capital gains.

Before going into the detailed processes involved it may be helpful to explain precisely what is achieved by making a loss claim. When a loss is 'relieved', this means that the loss is being used to extinguish an equivalent amount of income which has already been taxed or which would have been taxed in the future. If the loss is being applied against current income, any tax already paid on that income, e.g. tax deducted at source from dividends, will be repaid. If the loss is applied against past income then any tax paid on such income will be repaid together with, in certain circumstances, an interest supplement. This latter point makes it particularly attractive to use loss relief to recover tax paid in earlier years. If the loss is carried forward to be relieved against future income, then no tax will be paid on such income as is extinguished by the losses.

Before looking at the details of the legislation covering loss relief, it is essential that the reader has a clear picture of the structure of a personal tax computation and in particular, of the stages in a computation where the various forms of loss relief are applied. The Sections referred to will be described in detail at the end of the computation. An outline computation is shown below:

Personal Tax Computation – 1992/93

Schedule D I (trading profits)		£XXXX
Less, Capital Allowances		XXXX
		XXXX
Less, TRADING LOSSES B/FWD (Section 385) OR TRADING LOSSES B/BACK (Section 388) (TERMINAL LOSSES)		XXXX
		XXXX
Add, Other Income		
Schedule D III (interest received gross)		XXXX
Schedule A (rental income)		XXXX
Schedule F		XXXX
Building Society Interest		XXXX
Plus any other taxable income (listed)		XXXX
		XXXX
Less, Annual charges:		
Mortage Interest	£XXX	
Charitable Covenants	XXX	
		XXX
Statutory total income		XXXX

Less, CURRENT TRADING LOSSES (Section 380) OR TRADING LOSSES B/BACK (Section 381) (LOSSES IN A NEW BUSINESS)	£XXXX
	XXXX
Less, Personal Allowances	XXXX
Taxable income	£XXXX

In the following descriptions of the various sections, the reader is advised to refer to the above layout.

Section 380

This provides that the trading loss for an accounting year ending in a particular tax year **may** be relieved against the **total income** (as shown in the above layout) for that same tax year. Strictly, the law requires that the trading loss for an accounting year be allocated to the tax years concerned. However, by concession the Revenue permit the loss to 'belong', for tax purposes, to the tax year in which the loss making year ends.

The above concession does **not** apply during the first three tax years of the life of a business nor in its last year. In these cases, the 'strict' basis must be applied. The treatment of losses in the early years of a business (apart from Section 381 – see below) is a horrendously complex area and beyond the scope of this book. Sufficient to say that, whereas profits can be assessed more than once in a new business, losses, in general, are not allowed more than once!

Where, having applied the loss in this fashion, there remains some unused loss, then this may be carried forward and be relieved against the **total income** of the immediately following tax year **only**. The following points should be noted:

- The loss is applied against **total** income – i.e. **after** deducting annual charges and **before** deducting personal allowances. This latter point is most important since personal allowances (including the married couple's allowance) can only be used where there is income from which to deduct them. If there is **no** income (because loss relief has wiped it out) then the personal allowances are lost. They cannot be carried forward. An unused loss, on the other hand, may be carried forward indefinitely.

6

- Prior to 6 April 1990, a trading loss sustained by one spouse could be set against the income of the other spouse. From that date, however, husbands and wives are treated as separate persons and this facility is no longer available.
- Where a husband has claimed loss relief and his income is then too small to absorb any or part of the married couple's allowance, the unused allowance may be transferred to his wife.
- In most cases, the option to use the loss under Section 380 for the second year is not taken since the basis period for that year produced a loss and, therefore, the income is zero.

Example

A trader in business for many years who makes up accounts to 31 December each year has the following results:

31 December 1991	Profit	£20,000
31 December 1992	Loss	35,000
31 December 1993	Profit	45,000

1992/93

Profits assessed – preceding year	£20,000
Loss making year **ended** in 1992/93	
Section 380 claim	35,000
Assessable income	NIL
Balance of loss carried forward	15,000

Tax payable

Any tax paid on £20,000 is refunded.

1993/94

Assessment – year ended 31 December 1992 NIL (a loss)

Loss brought forward cannot be used – no income.

The only situation in which the £15,000 of unused losses would be used under Section 380 for 1993/94 is where the taxpayer had income from other sources chargeable for that year equal to the loss of £15,000 plus any available personal allowances for the year. Otherwise personal allowances would be 'wasted'.

Carry forward loss under Section 385

Where, after the second possible year of a Section 380 claim, there is still some unrelieved loss – £15,000 in the above example – such loss is available for carry forward indefinitely against Schedule D I income (trading profits) **only**.

It must be applied against the first trading profits earned in the future. In the above example the assessments would continue:

1994/95

Preceding year 31 December 1993	£45,000
Less, losses brought forward Section 385	15,000
Assessable	£30,000
Less, personal allowances	3,445
Taxable	£26,555
£ 2,000 @ 20%	£ 400
21,700 @ 25%	5,425
2,855 @ 40%	1,142
	£ 6,967

Where a loss is brought forward under Section 385, it can **only** eliminate trading income and thus, where the brought forward loss exceeds the trading income for the year to which it is brought forward, then the unused balance of the loss is carried forward to future years. If there is other income for this year, it will, after the deduction of personal allowances, be taxed in the normal way.

A common decision which has to be made is whether to claim the loss against current income (Section 380) or to carry it forward against future income (Section 385). Where the current year's income is modest and would be extinguished by personal allowances then clearly no claim would be made under Section 380. Even where, after using personal allowances, there is a modest tax bill to be paid, it may be advisable not to claim under Section 380 and leave the loss to be carried forward against future trading income.

This approach relies on reasonable knowledge about future profits. By utilising otherwise unusable personal allowances, it generally results in a lower tax bill over a period of three years. Much depends on whether the taxpayer is willing, and able, to pay some tax now in the knowledge that tax will be saved in the future, perhaps at the higher rate.

Losses in new businesses – Section 381

Where a loss arises in any of the first **four** tax years of a business's life, the loss for a particular year may be **carried back** and set against a taxpayer's **total income** (as previously defined) for the three tax years prior to that in which the loss was sustained, starting with the earliest year and working forward. This is a most valuable form of relief for new businesses and the following points should be noted:

- In this form of relief the concessionary basis of treating the loss does **not** apply. It is the **actual** loss sustained **during** the tax year which is the basis of the claim. This may have to be calculated by apportioning the results of two **accounting** years into the tax year concerned, netting profits against losses if necessary.
- The relief is similar to that given by Section 380 in that the loss is applied against all income (after deducting annual charges) and prior to 6 April 1990, the claim could be extended to a spouse's income. A typical beneficiary of this form of relief would be an individual who has been a high salary earner, paying higher rate taxes for some years, who sets up in business and initially sustains trading losses. Remember these losses could be increased (or occasioned) by capital allowances on equipment bought to start up the business. Such expenditure tends to be high at this point in a business's life.
- Remember that, since the relief is first applied to the earliest year, the tax recovered is three years old with three years' interest supplement paid with the refund. This can result in very substantial repayments being received.

Terminal losses – Section 388

To complete the coverage of losses it is necessary to consider one form of relief which it is hoped no readers of this book will ever have to be concerned with.

Clearly, when a business ceases to trade there is nowhere for the losses to be carried forward to! The relief is thus retrospective. When a business ceases to trade, any losses sustained in the last 12 **months** of trading, together with any **unused** capital allowances for this period are added together and form a claim for terminal losses. The amount of such losses can be carried back and relieved against the **trading profits only** (after deducting capital allowances) for the three years of assessment preceding that in which the business ceased trading, starting with the **latest** year and working back.

Where the amount of the terminal loss exceeds the available profits in the three previous years, then unfortunately the balance of the terminal loss claim is unusable and is lost.

There is one planning point in this area which must not be overlooked. This arises where a substantial loss occurs in the **second** last year of assessment and, shortly after the cessation, the erstwhile trader obtains employment.

It could be advantageous to make a claim under Section 380, carry the loss forward to the following year, when wages are being earned, and set the loss against these wages, obtaining a refund of some of the tax being paid on this.

Transfer of a business to a limited company – Section 386

Where a sole trader or a partnership transfers a going concern to a limited company solely or mainly for shares in that company, any accumulated unused losses being carried forward at that point may be used by the previous owner(s) of the former business against **any** income they derive in any future tax year (throughout which they continue to hold the shares) from the company in the form of dividends, salary or bonuses. Such losses must be applied against the **first** such income from the company and **cannot** be relieved against any other income from other sources, nor can they be used by the company. Note that unrelieved capital allowances may not be included in losses carried forward under Section 386.

The role of capital allowances in loss claims – Section 383

Where a claim is made under S. 380 (or S. 381) the amount of the loss may be extended (or a profit may be converted into a loss) by the addition of any capital allowances which may be available for the basis period corresponding to the loss making year. Thus, where there is a loss for the year ended 31 December 1992, a claim under S. 380 may be made for the tax year 1992/93 and the loss may be increased by the amount of capital allowances available by reference to the year ended 31 December 1992.

Had no loss claim been appropriate, these capital allowances would have been available, on a normal preceding year basis, for the tax year 1993/94. Just as a S. 380 claim allows the loss to be accelerated into an earlier year, S. 383 allows capital allowances to be similarly treated.

Section 72 of the Finance Act 1991

For tax years 1991/92 onwards, where a loss claim under Section 380 exceeds the income for the year of the claim, the excess loss may be set against chargeable capital gains for that year.

A most important final thought on losses. Throughout this chapter it will be noticed that all of the reliefs mentioned are available against the taxpayer's **personal** income. Some provide quite spectacular reductions in the taxpayer's bills or refunds (with interest) of tax previously paid. This is important to remember as we are about to go on to look at the tax implications of trading as a limited company. Here we will find that any losses made by a company are **locked into** that company and can **never** be used to reduce or recover tax paid on **personal** income. This is a most important factor to consider when deciding whether, initially, you really should start the business as a company.

This point is especially important where the business is likely to trade at a loss in the first few years until it becomes established. By forming a company you are denied the opportunity of making a claim under Section 381 (carry back of early losses) which is by far the most helpful piece of legislation in this whole area of losses.

The Inland Revenue publication IR 28 – *Tax and your business, Starting in business* – contains useful information on loss reliefs.

7 Limited companies – Corporation tax

Partnership or sole trader □ Limited company □ Corporation tax layout □ Charge to corporation tax □ Basis of assessment □ Computation of total profits □ Treatment of investment income □ Annual charges on income □ Accounting for income tax □ Associated companies and length of accounting period □ Marginal rate of tax □ Summary of the imputation system □ Owners/directors of a company □ Comparing different business structures □ Close companies □ Corporation tax losses □ Appendix

This chapter will deal with the taxation implications arising from trading in the form of a limited company and at the end of it will hopefully leave the reader with the answer to what is probably the most common question posed by someone about to set up a business – should I trade as a sole trader/partnership or as a limited company?

While this book obviously concentrates on the taxation implications of such a decision, it is most important to take into account all of the commercial considerations involved in the decision. It will be useful, therefore, before dealing with the taxation aspects, to consider the non-taxation implications of trading as a company as opposed to running the business as a sole trader or partnership. The following two sections summarise the main considerations involved.

Partnership or sole trader

1 Financing the business

The initial finance for running the business will be subscribed by the owner or partners. In the case of partnerships the capital would be subscribed in whatever varying sums the partners agree to provide. Where these amounts are significantly disparate, as between various partners, such differences can be rewarded by crediting to the partners, as an initial allocation of profits, interest on the capital provided at an agreed rate per annum. Generally capital can be withdrawn without creating any problems (provided funds are available).

Additional capital may, of course, be borrowed from various lenders including banks. A good business plan is essential for this purpose.

2 Liability of owner or partners

The owners will have unlimited liability and in the case of a partnership, the liability of each partner will be 'joint and several'. This means that **each** partner can be held liable for the **whole debts** of the partnership. This would only be a problem where the business is likely to incur large liabilities at any time. If the business does get into financial difficulties, the effect of unlimited liability can be quite devastating and the owners could lose all of their personal assets. Legal advice should be sought in an effort to avoid the worst effects of such an occurrence. Typical action would be to put a house in the name of a spouse. In certain types of businesses, for example professional firms (including consultancies) the risk involved takes the form of claims for negligence and the owners must ensure that adequate professional indemnity insurance cover is obtained.

3 Conduct of the business

In the case of a partnership, the detailed regulations for running the business – salaries; drawings; interest; share of profits; cheque signatories; procedures on changes in partnership (persons leaving or joining); and any specific rules peculiar to the business – would be contained in a partnership agreement. Such a written agreement is not required in law (the Partnership Act would apply in the absence of a written document) but it is **most advisable** to have a deed drawn up by a solicitor. In the case of a sole trader, no such written rules are necessary. A bank account should be opened in the business name.

4 Records and Financial Accounts

There are no statutory rules governing either the nature of the records or the form and content of any Accounts produced (*but* see VAT later). However, it would be an odd partnership agreement which did not require annual accounts to be produced. In addition, the Inland Revenue would insist on properly prepared accounts. A sole trader or a partnership has no obligation to appoint an auditor or have an audit conducted – although again, any partnership agreement would make reference to this. Any audit conducted would not be under the very stringent requirements which apply to limited companies.

No returns need be submitted to the Registrar and the accounts of the business do not require to be filed for public scrutiny.

Limited company

1 Financing the business

The initial capital is subscribed in the form of share capital, these shares being allotted in whatever allocation is agreed. The total amount of such share capital can be modest and this is most common. The bulk of the finance required is usually provided by directors in the form of loans. These have the advantage that they can be withdrawn as soon as the company is in funds. Share capital can be difficult to withdraw, being a form of permanent capital (although it is not impossible to do so). Any business expenses paid by the directors before the company has any funds can be treated as directors' loans, to be repaid as above. Additional share capital in a company may be raised under the Business Expansion Scheme, where the subscribers, who obtain tax relief on up to £40,000 p.a., are not involved in the running of the business.

2 Liability

The basic idea of a limited company is that the liability of the shareholders is limited to the nominal value of the shares they have subscribed for and, therefore, the shareholders will have no liability for the debts of the company. This can often be illusory and if the company were to approach a lender for funds, the lender would insist on personal guarantees from the directors – such as a house as security. In the case of newly formed companies, such guarantees would be insisted upon. Where the funding is mainly in the form of directors' loans then this is at risk along with other creditors of the company.

3 Conduct of the business

The rules for running a company are contained in the Articles of Association which every company must have drawn up. A specimen set of these is contained in the Companies Act, 1985 and most companies adopt these, modified where appropriate. These rules broadly cover some of the items which would be included in a partnership agreement but they do have statutory authority. A ready formed company may be purchased for about £200 (in some cases more cheaply).

4 Records and Financial Accounts

There are very strict statutory rules (with penalties for non-compliance) governing the nature and content of both the day-to-day records to be maintained and the annual accounts to be produced.

In addition an Annual Return must be furnished to the Registrar of Companies containing a modified version of the company's Financial Accounts together with details of the shareholders and directors. An independent auditor **must** be appointed and he reports both to the shareholders and to the Registrar. He charges a fee! There have, in recent times, been moves to abolish the need for a statutory audit in the case of small companies but nothing has come of this to date. An important difference in a company is that it is a separate legal entity from the shareholders/directors (who are simply employees of the company) and it cannot be treated as a cash box from which cash is withdrawn willy nilly (other than loan capital). Withdrawal of cash usually creates tax problems.

The remainder of this chapter will be devoted to the taxation of companies and will cover in detail the areas which will be of most interest to those running small businesses. These would tend to be largely the position of directors/shareholders in relation to the company and the way in which the taxation of companies differs from the way in which other businesses are taxed. The reader is referred to Appendix 1 of Chapter 1 which sets out the important differences, from a tax point of view, between the alternative types of business structure. As we go through this chapter, these differences will become more readily understandable. Already we have seen, in Chapter 6, that there is clearly an advantage in **not** having a company if the business makes losses, especially in its earliest years. In Chapter 3 we saw that there can be considerable tax savings achieved when a business ceases. It might, therefore, be tax efficient to start the business as a sole trader and after a period of five years, convert it to a company, thus creating a cessation.

Before looking in detail at how the system of corporation tax operates, it may be helpful to see what a corporation tax computation looks like. As the reader works through this chapter reference should be made to the pro forma layout provided here which incorporates all of the areas covered in the ensuing text.

Corporation tax layout

CAP from *to*

		Income Tax
Schedule D I	£	
Less, Losses b/f	£	
Schedule D III	£	
Schedule D IV & V	£	
Schedule D VI	£	
Schedule A	£	
UFII – from which income tax has been deducted (Gross)	£	£
Building Society Interest (Gross)	£	£
Chargeable gains	£	
Less, current trading losses	£	
Less charges paid in CAP	£	( )
Profits chargeable to CT **I**	£	£
Add, FII (Gross figure)	£	
Total profits of company P	£	
CT chargeable:		
Financial year @	£	
Financial year @	£	

Less, taper relief (if appropriate)	£
Less income tax suffered (on UFII)	£
CT ultimately payable	£

Subject to any ACT paid – deducted after taper relief see Expanded layout.

Expanded layout where ACT is involved

CT chargeable:		
Financial year @		£
Financial year @		£
Less taper relief (if appropriate)		£
		£
Less, ACT (Advance Corporation Tax):		
Dividends paid (gross)	£	
Less, FII (gross)	£	
ACT paid @ 25% on	£	
	£	£
Restricted to:		
(if appropriate)		
25% × 'I' (chargeable income)	£	£
Surplus ACT	£	
Mainstream CT		£
Less income tax suffered		£
CT ultimately payable		£

See Imputation System, later in the chapter, for coverage of ACT.

Key to abbreviations used in the layout

- CT – Corporation tax
- ACT – Advance corporation tax
- CAP – Chargeable accounting period
- FII – Franked investment income
- UFII – Unfranked investment income

These terms are fully explained in the remainder of this chapter.

Charge to corporation tax

Corporation tax is a tax on companies which are defined as 'any body corporate or unincorporated association but does not include a partnership or local authority'. Corporation tax is chargeable on companies (both limited and unlimited and extends to clubs of all kinds. (Section 831.)

Corporation tax (CT) is predominantly a residence based tax. A UK resident company is required to pay CT on its 'profits' (see below) whether arising in the UK or elsewhere and whether or not remitted to the UK. Relief would be given in respect of foreign tax paid.

Section 6 charges corporation tax on the **profits** of a company. These consist of the company's income from all sources, including capital gains. CT is not charged on Franked Investment Income (FII) i.e. dividends received from UK resident companies. The term **Income** (I) in the context of corporation tax means **Profits** (P) less FII.

Basis of Assessment

Corporation tax is generally charged on the profits (as defined above) of the company's own accounting period. The rates of corporation tax are fixed for each **financial year** (the 12 months ending 31 March). A financial year is described by the calendar year in which it **commenced**; thus the financial year ended 31 March 1993 is known as the FY 1992. The rates for the most recent years are shown at the end of this chapter. Where a company's accounting period straddles a 31 March then the profits are apportioned to the two financial years concerned, on a time basis, and CT charged on each part at the rates applicable to the respective financial years.

Note that the preceding year basis applicable to Schedule D I has no relevance for companies nor does the method of identifying tax years e.g. 1991/92 (other than for fixing rates of ACT – see Imputation System).

Chargeable accounting periods

Normally a company makes up accounts for a 12 month period to its accounting reference date. However, in some situations, it may prepare them for a period which is longer or shorter than 12 months. Section 12 contains rules which determine accounting periods for tax purposes. A corporation tax chargeable accounting period (CAP) begins when a company first comes within the charge to corporation tax (normally the commencement of trading) or immediately after the end of the previous CAP. A CAP ends with the earliest of the following events:

- The end of 12 months from the start of a CAP
- The company's normal accounting date
- Cessation of trading
- Beginning or ceasing to be UK resident
- Company ceasing to be within the charge to UK tax

A company requires permission from the Registrar of Companies to extend its accounting period. Where a company has a 15 month accounting period for accounts purposes, then this is split into a 12 month and a three month CAP for CT purposes.

Dates for payment of CT

A company is required to pay its corporation tax bill nine months after the end of its accounting period. This is a considerable disadvantage when compared with a sole trader or partnership, who are allowed up to 20 months to pay their first instalment of tax (see Chapter 3).

Computation of total profits

Beginning with the operating profit shown by the Profit and Loss Account, it is necessary to make adjustments to this figure to arrive at the Schedule D Case I figure. The main adjustments are, in general, exactly those which apply in arriving at the adjusted profit figure for unincorporated businesses (see Chapter 2). The aim is to eliminate all non-trading income such as interest received, dividends, income from property and capital gains. Certain items of trading income which have suffered tax at source e.g. patent royalties are also removed.

The main items in the adjusting process which are peculiar to limited companies are:

- Capital allowances are treated as a trading adjustment i.e. deducted as part of the adjustment process. Note that where an accounting period is less than 12 months, the WDA is scaled down to the appropriate number of months. Where it is more than 12 months, the WDA is calculated in two steps – first a full WDA and then a WDA based on the remaining months is calculated on the reduced balance. Any private use element of an asset used by a director/employee is ignored in computing WDA (see Chapters 4 and 9).
- Appropriations of profit peculiar to companies – dividends, transfers to reserves, amounts written off, goodwill – are never allowed as deductions.
- Annual charges which are paid net of tax are never allowed in arriving at the Schedule D I figure. (See annual charges below.)
- Directors' salaries are allowed, provided they are reasonable payment for the work done.

Treatment of investment income

While **all** items of investment income are removed from the profit in arriving at the Schedule D I figure, they are **all**, with the important exception of FII, chargeable to corporation tax and, therefore, included in the CT computation (see CT working sheet layout earlier in this chapter). Each item presents individual problems and these are dealt with below.

Unfranked Investment Income (UFII)

The following types of income are received by companies under deduction of basic rate income tax:

- Loan Interest
- Debenture Interest
- Patent Royalties
- Building Society Interest.

The **gross** amount of such items must be included in the CT computation and the income suffered at source will, in general, be treated as a tax credit against the CT liability. (See accounting for income tax later.) Note carefully that certain items of investment income received **gross** by companies e.g. bank deposit interest, are not UFII and thus carry **no** tax credit.

Dividends received

Dividends received from non-UK resident companies are chargeable to UK CT under Schedule D V and are, therefore, included in the CT computation (relief will be given for foreign tax suffered).

Dividends received from UK companies (Franked Investment Income – FII) are **not** chargeable to UK CT, since they have already suffered CT in the hands of the paying company having been paid out of **post-tax** profits. They must **never**, therefore, be included in the CT computation. The **gross** amount, which is what the phrase FII means in legislation, **must** however, be taken into account to determine whether the company's **total income** is less than £250,000 or more than £1,250,000 – the thresholds at which the rates of tax change (see Appendix). Thus, while FII is not charged to CT, its presence can have an effect on the rate of tax which the company will pay on its **other** income.

The tax suffered at source in receiving FII has a peculiar role in CT. It can **never** be treated as a tax credit in reducing the CT liability (since the income giving rise to it is not itself included in the CT computation). The credit does have a vital role to play in the cash flow position of a company (see accounting for advance corporation tax (ACT) below).

Chargeable gains

Capital gains realised are taxed at the same rate as the rest of a company's income. Any gains may be reduced by the amount of capital losses sustained in the same accounting period, or by any such losses brought forward. It is possible that the presence of a gain in a particular accounting period could push the company's income into a higher rate band, therefore, the timing of realisations of assets giving rise to gains should be carefully considered.

Annual charges on income

These comprise any yearly interest, annuity or other annual payment from which basic rate income tax has been deducted by the paying company. Those most commonly encountered are:

- Loan interest paid
- Debenture interest paid
- Patent royalties
- Charitable covenants
- Gift aid to charities (paid next of tax)

None of these items is allowed as a deduction in arriving at the company's Schedule D I profit figure.

As indicated, all of these items are paid by companies **net** of basic rate income tax. The amount shown in the profit and loss account will always be the **gross** amount and it is important to remember that income tax has been deducted. As you will see from the corporation tax working sheet layout, the **gross** amount of annual charges **actually paid** in the CAP is deducted from the **total profits**.

Payments which have been allowed as a deduction in arriving at the Schedule D I figure may not be treated as an annual charge. Note carefully that bank overdraft interest is a *trading expense* and **not** an annual charge.

Where the annual charges exceed the total profits, then the excess may be carried forward and set off against future trading profits, provided the excess consists of charges wholly and exclusively for the purpose of the trade (Section 390). Non-trade charges – the most common example being charitable covenants – can never be carried forward in this manner.

Accounting for income tax

While companies are not within the charge to income tax they do, as indicated above become involved with income tax in two ways:

---

1. Income tax is retained when paying annual charges. This income tax will require to be remitted to the collector of taxes.
2. Income tax is suffered by the company when it receives certain types of UFII.

The company will obtain relief for the income tax suffered under point 2 above by:

(a) Having it set off against any income tax which it is required to pay in respect of income tax retained on paying annual charges as described at 2 above.
(b) Setting it against the company's liability to CT for the same CAP.

(c) Where there is no CT liability, any income tax suffered and not relieved under (a) or (b) will be repaid to the company once the assessment has been agreed at nil with the Inspector of Taxes.

The above process describes what will happen, taking a CAP as a whole, at the end of that CAP. Note that if the income tax suffered on UFII exceeds the amount retained by the company on paying charges, the resultant credit is either set against the CT liability or repaid. Whereas if the amount that has been retained exceeds the amount suffered, the difference will represent income tax which has simply been paid (or will be paid shortly).

The company is required to account for any income tax retained – taking account of any tax suffered – on a quarterly basis during each CAP. The detail is entered on form CT 61 and the completed form submitted to the Collector of Taxes within 14 days of the end of each quarter. The quarters referred to are the calendar quarters:

Three months ended	31 March
Three months ended	30 June
Three months ended	30 September
Three months ended	31 December

Where the company's CAP does not coincide with one of the above dates the company will have an additional settlement period, making five in all.

For example, if a company's accounting period ended on 31 August, it would have a settlement period running from 1 September to 30 September, then the above periods until 30 June, and finally a period from 1 July to 31 August. In all cases any tax due must be remitted within fourteen days of the end of the settlement period.

The preceding paragraphs have set out the manner in which a company's taxable income is arrived at and have touched on the method of charging corporation tax. There are now two crucial areas which must be looked at to complete the main coverage of company taxation:

1. The computation of the amount of corporation tax charged. This will involve using the various rates in force from time to time.
2. The system of corporation tax presently operated in the UK –

known as the **imputation system**. It is important to grasp the basic principles involved in order to understand some of the decisions to be taken on how to extract funds from the company.

Associated companies and length of accounting period

It should be noted that the thresholds of £250,000 and £1,250,000 shown in the appendix to this chapter refer to companies with no associated companies and whose CAP is exactly 12 months. Where there are associated companies – a company is associated where it is controlled by another company or is under common control by an individual with another company – or the CAP is less than 12 months, then the thresholds are scaled down accordingly. If there are **five** associated companies, the thresholds for **each** company become £50,000 and £250,000. If a CAP for a single company (no associates) is six months, then the thresholds become £125,000 and £625,000.

Example

JP Ltd and IP Ltd are associated companies (controlled by the same person) with the following profits (trading income only):

JP Ltd	nine months to 31 March 1993	£470,000
IP Ltd	six months to 31 March 1993	60,000

What is the status of each company for CT purposes?

JP Ltd is a **large** company – paying CT at 33% on all of its income since £470,000 is greater than £1,250,000 × ½ (two associated companies) × 9/12 (nine months) = £468,750.
IP is a **small** company paying tax at 25% since its profits are less than £250,000 × ½ (two associated companies) × 6/12 (six months) = £62,500.

Marginal rate of tax

The rate structure for CT has an implicit marginal rate applicable to profits between £250,001 and £1,249,999. This is currently

35 per cent. It is most important for companies to be aware that they are paying this rate on some of their income. Any deductible expenditure, such as pension contributions, becomes very tax efficient.

Where a company's **profits** (P) exceeds £250,000 but does not exceed £1,250,000, the company will pay some of its CT at a marginal rate of tax. This results from the operation of *taper relief* and has the effect of making the company's **overall** rate of tax higher than 25 per cent but lower than 33 per cent. The relief works by taxing the company's **income** (I) at the higher rate – 33 per cent – and deducting the answer to the following calculation:

$$(M - P) \times I/P \times \text{Relevant fraction (see appendix)}$$

Where: **M** = Upper Threshold – currently £1,250,000 – scaled down if there are associated companies and/or if the CAP is less than 12 months.
P = Income from **all** sources including FII (gross).
I = Taxable profits – i.e. 'P' excluding FII.

Note that the presence of FII can change the status of a company despite the fact that this income is not charged to CT.

The reader should not attempt to rationalise this formula, but rather concentrate on its effect!

Example

The following figures will be used to demonstrate the application of taper relief and explain the implicit marginal rate of CT described earlier.

Assume XY Ltd has trading profits of £250,000 for the CAP 12 months ended 31 March 1993. We can calculate the additional CT which would be payable if the profits had increased to £350,000 for the same CAP. There are **no** associated companies.

Profits = £250,000 – small company – CT @ 25%		£62,500
Profits = £350,000 – intermediate company:		
CT = £350,000 @ 33%	£115,500	
Less, Taper relief:		
(£1,250,000 – £350,000)		
× 1/1 × 1/50	£18,000	
(I and P are the same – no FII)		
		£97,500
Extra CT on extra profits of £100,000		£35,000
(i.e. an effective rate of 35%)		

Tax of £97,500 on £350,000 is an effective rate of 27.85 per cent (higher than 25 per cent and lower than 33 per cent). The total CT comprises:

£250,000 @ 25% **plus** £100,000 @ 35%

Thus the profits over £250,000 attract CT at 35 per cent.

An important effect of this phenomenon arises where a company buys a controlling interest in another company or an individual who already controls an existing company, buys a controlling interest in a second company – thus creating an associated company situation. This could affect the rate of tax payable by the acquiring (or first) company. This can be most damaging where the second company has virtually no income in its first year after acquisition. See illustration below.

Illustration

Mr Glugg owns 95 per cent of the share capital of Drains Ltd (his wife owns the remaining 5 per cent). The company is making profits of approximately £150,000 per annum. On 1 April 1992, he decides to acquire, at an attractive price, a controlling interesting in Gunge Ltd, a company which is barely breaking even, but with an excellent customer base. Assume that the trading results of each company for the year ended 31 March 1993 were:

Drains Ltd	£200,000
Gunge Ltd	£1,000

As a result of the acquisition, the companies are now associated companies, both being controlled by Mr Glugg. The threshold for the small company rate becomes £250,000 × ½ = £125,000 (large company threshold is £1,250,000 × ½ = £625,000). Drains Ltd is now an **intermediate** company. Prior to the acquisition of Gunge Ltd by Mr Glugg, it had been a **small** company.

CT due by each company:

Drains Ltd £200,000 @ 33%	£66,000	
Less, Taper relief – (£625,000 – £200,000) × 1/1 × 1/50 =	8,500	
		£57,500
Gunge Ltd (small company – less than ½ × £200,000) £1,000 @ 25%		250
Total CT payable by two companies		£57,750
If, instead of acquiring the share capital of Gunge Ltd, Mr Glugg had arranged for Drains Ltd to acquire the business, assets and customers of Gunge Ltd, there would only be **one** company (no associated company) earning total profits of £201,000 making it a small company. CT @ 25% =		50,250
Additional tax as a result of acquiring shares of Gunge Ltd		£ 7,500

The additional tax arises because Drain Ltd's threshold is halved to £125,000 and is now paying CT on £75,000 of its income at 35 per cent instead of 25 per cent:

10% × £75,000 = £7,500

While there may be excellent commercial reasons for acquiring the share capital of Gunge Ltd, the taxation implications should be considered.

The operation of the imputation system can sometimes be extremely complex and it is unlikely that small companies will become involved in such complexities. The coverage has therefore been reduced to the minimum required to gain an appreciation of the system. This is summarised below.

Summary of the imputation system

- Corporation tax is payable on a company's chargeable income which comprises all of its income (excluding dividends received from other UK companies) less annual charges plus capital gains.

- Dividends paid to shareholders have 'imputed' to them a tax credit equal to the current basic rate of income tax. For the last five income tax years up to 1992/93 this amounted to 25/75 of the dividend. This satisfies the shareholder's liability to basic rate tax. The illustrations in this book use an ACT rate of 25/75.
- The company is required to make a payment to the collector of taxes equal to 25/75 of the dividend. This represents a payment on account of the company's Corporation Tax liability for the year *in which the dividend is paid*. This payment is called 'advance corporation tax' (ACT). It is *not* an additional or separate tax but merely a payment on account of the ultimate corporation tax liability. It therefore has important cash flow implications.
- ACT must be paid within 14 days of the end of the quarter in which the dividend is paid. The information is submitted on Form CT 61. The quarters referred to are calendar quarters but where a company's accounting date does not coincide with the calendar quarter, an extra payment period will arise. This method is exactly the same as applies to quarterly income tax settlements described earlier in this chapter.
- Interaction – ACT/FII (dividends from UK companies). The tax credit associated with dividends received from other UK companies *cannot* be used against the company's corporation tax liability (as happens in a personal computation). The FII tax credit may only be used to reduce any ACT otherwise payable by the company. Thus FII tax credits *cannot reduce* the company's corporation tax liability. It merely permits *less* ACT to be paid *now* and *more* MCT (mainstream corporation tax) to be paid *later*. The total corporation tax bill is *unchanged*. However, the cash flow is obviously improved. While only a minority of small companies would be regular recipients of dividends, most would, at some stage, be likely to pay dividends. An awareness of the tax consequences is therefore important.

Illustration

The following example will demonstrate the manner in which the imputation system operates.

A Ltd – Year ended 31 March 1993

Trading profit	£145,000
UK dividends received (actual amount)	3,000
Dividend paid during year	30,000

A Ltd's total income comprises:

Trading profits	£145,000
FII – gross figure = £3,000 × 4/3 (received net of 25% tax)	4,000
	£149,000

A Ltd is therefore a small company – income less than £250,000 CT payable on **chargeable** income (not FII)

£145,000 @ 25%		£36,250
Less, ACT:		
Dividend paid £30,000 – ACT = 1/3 =	£10,000	
Less, tax credit of FII – 25% × £4,000	1,000	
ACT actually paid	9,000	9,000
Balance of CT payable nine months after accounting period (this is called *Mainstream Corporation Tax* – MCT)		£27,250

It is most important to note that the ACT has not altered the CT bill; it has only altered the timing of the payment of the bill.

The following points should be considered:

- Had the company paid no dividends and received no FII it would have paid **all** of its corporation tax **nine** months after the end of its accounting period – 1 January 1994.
- Had it paid the above dividend but received no FII, it would have paid £10,000 of its CT bill, fourteen days after the end of the quarter in which it paid its dividend (this could have been as early as 14 July 1992 – if the dividend was paid in quarter to 30 June 1992). The balance of its CT – £26,250 – would be payable on 1 January 1994. This confirms the nature of ACT – it is indeed CT paid in **advance**! In this case eighteen months in advance!
- The presence of the FII has allowed the company to reduce its payment of ACT and thus allowed the company to retain an extra £1,000 of cash for an extra eighteen months. Thus FII has an important cash flow implication.

Note:
The above ACT of £9,000 can be arrived at by taking gross dividend paid (called a Franked Payment) of £40,000 (£30,000 × 4/3) and subtracting the FII of £4,000 = £36,000 and taking 25% = £9,000.

There is one remaining problem associated with ACT and that is the matter of surplus ACT. While it is unlikely to affect very many small companies, when it does arise it can cause some difficulty.

While a company can normally treat any ACT paid as a payment on account of its CT liability, there is a limit placed on the amount which may be deducted in arriving at the MCT. The maximum deduction permitted is 25 per cent of the company's chargeable income and in a small company this is, of course, equal to the amount of CT charged on its income. Thus the ACT can reduce the MCT to nil. However, what if the amount of ACT paid on dividends paid during an accounting period is greater than the company's corporation tax bill for that period? This can easily happen where a good trading year with high profits is followed by a modest year, during which a large dividend is paid out of last year's profits. The surplus ACT arising in this situation can either be:

- carried back and treated as a payment on account of any accounting period commencing in the previous six years. Since the CT bills for these years have already been paid in full, the application of additional ACT to these years creates an overpayment which is repaid by the Inland Revenue. Each year is subject to a maximum ACT figure of 25 per cent of the income.
- carried forward and treated as a payment on account of the CT of any future year. This means that profits can be earned in the future on which no new CT will be payable since it has already been paid in an earlier year. Until ACT can be relieved in the future it represents an additional tax burden on the company.

The following illustration shows how the CT liability of a typical small company would be calculated and how it would be settled.

Pat McAuley Ltd, a distributor of dog foods, produces the following information in relation to its 12 month accounting period ending on 31 March 1993:

Trading profits (adjusted for taxation)	£120,000
Rental income	6,000
Building Society Interest (received 10/9/92)	4,000
(£4,000 is gross figure – actual receipt £3,000)	
Loan Interest paid (20 June 1992)	3,000
(£3,000 is gross figure – actual payment £2,250)	
Dividend paid (28 December 1992)	15,000

Corporation Tax Computation – 12 months ended 31 March 1993

		Income tax
Schedule D I	£120,000	
Schedule A	6,000	
Building Society Interest	4,000	£1,000
	130,000	1,000
Less, Annual Charge – Loan Interest	3,000	(750)
Chargeable Income (No FII)	£127,000	£ 250 IT suffered
CT £127,000 @ 25% (small company rate)	£31,750	
Less, ACT – Dividend paid £15,000 × 1/3	5,000	
	£26,750	
Less Income Tax suffered at source	250	
Mainstream CT ultimately payable	£26,500	

Of great importance to the owners is the question – when are the various bits of tax paid? This is clearly of great importance when planning cash flow.

First, the easy one. The mainstream CT is always payable nine months after the end of the accounting period. Thus £26,500 is due on 1 January 1994.

The ACT of £5,000 is payable fourteen days after the end of the calendar quarter in which the dividend was paid. The dividend of £15,000 was paid on 28 December 1992 – in the quarter ended 31 December 1992 and, therefore, the ACT of £5,000 is payable on 14 January 1993. Note that had this dividend been paid early in January 1993, the ACT would not have been payable until 14 April 1993, thus improving the cash flow position.

Now the tricky one – the income tax position. The loan interest of £2,250 (net) was paid on 20 June 1992 – in the quarter ended 30 June 1992 and therefore income tax of £750 would become payable on 14 July 1992. The building society interest of £3,000 (net) was received on 10 September 1992 – during the quarter ended 30 September 1992. The tax credit on this (£1,000) wipes out the tax due on the loan interest, which has already been paid on 14 July 1992. This permits a cash refund of this tax amounting to £750 on 14 October 1992. The remaining credit of £250 is deducted from the CT liability as shown in the above computation.

The coverage of corporation tax up to this point has concentrated on the position of the company. It would now be appropriate to look at the taxation position of the owners of a small company, that is, the shareholders who may, or may not be, directors or other persons involved in the day-to-day running of the business. It is only when this aspect has been studied that an informed decision can be made as to whether or not the business should be run as a company.

Owners/directors of a company

Unlike other forms of business structures, a company is a legal entity, quite separate from the individuals who own the share capital. It is also a separate taxable 'person'. Often those running small companies fail to make this distinction, losing sight of it in the pell-mell business of running a successful operation. This failure can lead to problems with the Inland Revenue, particularly that part of the Revenue dealing with PAYE (pay as you earn). (See Chapter 9.)

Shareholders

The position of those individuals who are shareholders but not involved in the management of the company or employed by it, is relatively straightforward. Their income comes in the form of dividends which are declared at a particular rate per share, this rate applying to all shares of the same class e.g. ordinary shares. These individuals will receive a dividend which has been deemed to have suffered basic rate tax (25 per cent) at source. Thus, if a dividend of £1,500 is received, this represents gross income of £2,000 from which income tax of £500 has been deducted. (This amount is paid by the company as ACT on the appropriate date.) If, after the inclusion of the £2,000 in the shareholder's personal tax computation, the taxable income is still within the basic rate band, then the shareholder will have no further tax to pay. If the shareholder is liable for higher rate tax – currently 40 per cent – then the additional tax due of 15 per cent will be payable on 1 December following the tax year in which the dividend was received. Finally, if the shareholder is not within the taxable range – with a very low income – then any tax suffered on the dividend will be refunded by the Revenue. Taxpayers with taxable income up to £2,000 will receive a repayment of 5 per cent.

Directors

It is almost certainly the case that most of the readers who are running small companies are very much involved, as directors, in the day-to-day running of the business and we will now turn to their taxation (and NIC) position.

First, a reminder that if the directors receive dividends, then their tax position is exactly as described above, with the company paying ACT fourteen days after the end of the quarter in which the dividends are paid.

The main form of reward for directors, who are simply employees of the company, tends to be in the form of salary and bonuses together with various 'perks' (see below). Such payments are assessable on the recipients under Schedule E, the basis for which is the actual amounts paid in the tax year. The problem with salaries and bonuses is that they create an immediate tax payment – PAYE tax being due on the 19th of each month on any payments made to directors up to the 5th of that month. In addition NIC (National Insurance Contributions) are payable at the same time, the current rates being (assuming a weekly salary of at least £190):

payable by employee – 2% × £54 plus 9% of next £351
(above £405 – nil)
payable by employer – 10.4% of **all** earnings
(no upper limit)
Where the employee is contracted out the rates are slightly lower (see p. 128).

A full table of NIC rates is given in an appendix at the end of Chapter 9.

It should be noted that the employer's contribution represents an additional cost to the employer in addition to any gross salary paid. NIC is not generally payable on benefits in kind i.e. 'perks' and these have consequently become an increasingly efficient method of rewarding employees. The later chapter on PAYE and other aspects of employment gives fuller coverage of the benefits position.

It becomes readily apparent that extracting funds from a company, either as dividends or especially as salaries can be costly and have an immediate adverse effect on cash flow. This contrasts markedly with the position in a business run as a sole trader or partnership.

Comparing different business structures

A useful exercise is to look at the overall effects of running the same business as either a limited company, or a sole trader or as a partnership of husband and wife, assuming varying levels of profit.

The following illustration assumes three alternative levels of profit:

£30,000 50,000 70,000	In the case of a limited company it has been assumed that the owner will require to take a gross salary of £27,180 p.a. to live on.

The first comparison is between a limited company and a sole trader where a married man is the owner. A husband and wife partnership will be considered later.

Profit of £30,000

		Limited company		*Sole trader*
Profit		£30,000		£30,000
Less, Salary	£27,180			
Emp'er NIC	2,826			
		30,006		
Chargeable to CT	Say	Nil	Charged to IT	£30,000

Corporation Tax		Nil	Income tax (paid later)	£ 6,091
PAYE		£ 5,404	NIC (class 4) "	941
NIC (employee)		1,699	Weekly Class 2 NIC	278
NIC (employer)		2,826		
(all paid monthly)				
Total Tax and NIC		£ 9,929		£ 7,310
Disposable Income				
Company		Nil		–
Director	£27,180		Owner	£30,000
Less PAYE & NIC	7,103		Less, Tax & NIC	7,310
		£20,077		
		£20,077		£22,690

At this level, a company does not look attractive. In addition, the sole trader can enjoy a considerable cash flow advantage in terms of dates of payment of tax. The company situation could be improved using benefits instead of salary (see Chapter 9).

Profit of £50,000

		Limited company		*Sole trader*
Profit		£50,000		£50,000
Less, Salary & NIC		30,006		–
Chargeable to CT	Say	20,000	Charged to IT	£45,000
Corporation Tax @ 25% (paid 9 months later)		£ 5,000	Income tax (paid later)	£14,091
PAYE		£ 5,404	NIC (class 4) (paid later)	941
NIC (employee)		1,699	Weekly Class 2 NIC	278
NIC (employer)		2,826		
(all paid monthly)				
Total Tax and NIC		£14,929		£15,310

Disposable Income				
Company		£15,000		
Director	£27,180		Owner	£50,000
Less PAYE & NIC	7,103		Less, Tax & NIC	15,310
		£20,007		
		£35,007		£34,690

At this level we are nearer a breakeven point both in terms of the total tax burden and the disposable income. There is still a considerable cash flow advantage for the sole trader who may not be required to pay the tax and Class 4 NIC until possibly twenty months after the accounting year, whereas the company will have to pay the PAYE and NIC monthly and the CT of £5,000 in nine months time. It must be remembered that, in the company situation, £15,000 of the disposable income is locked into the company and if it were to be put at the disposal of the owner there would be a tax charge whether it was taken as salary or dividends. At this level of income it may be the case that the company is in a better position to provide benefits for the director as an alternative to salary. If this were done there would be a saving on employer's NIC, since amounts assessed as benefits (excluding cars) do not generally attract NIC at the present time.

Profit of £70,000

		Limited company		*Sole trader*
Profit		£70,000		£70,000
Less, Salary & NIC		30,006		–
Chargeable to CT	Say	40,000	Charged to IT	£60,000
Corporation Tax @ 25% (paid 9 months later)		£10,000	Income Tax (paid later)	£22,091
PAYE		£ 5,404	NIC (class 4) (paid later)	941
NIC (employee)		1,699	Weekly Class 2 NIC	278
NIC (employer) (all paid monthly)		2,826		
Total Tax and NIC		£19,929		£23,310

7

Disposable Income				
Company		£30,000		
Director	£27,180		Owner	£70,000
Less PAYE & NIC	7,103		Less, Tax & NIC	23,310
		£20,007		
		£50,007		£46,690

At this level the overall tax burden is higher in the sole trader and the overall disposable income is higher in the company. However the sole trader still has a cash flow advantage for the reasons previously stated. In addition, in the company situation, £30,000 of the disposable income is locked into the company. Again, benefits could be used to reduce the employer's NIC charge. In this example and in the previous one, there is obviously an opportunity for the owners (directors) to take out additional amounts for their own use. This could be by way of salary (bonus) or dividend. Let us assume that £10,000 (gross) was taken and compare the effect if this were taken as salary or as a dividend:

	Salary			*Dividend*
Amount of payment	£10,000			£10,000
Additional PAYE (some @ 40%)	3,747	Both payable immediately	ACT payable 14 days after quarter	2,500
Additional NIC	1,040		(This is **not** additional tax but a payment to account of CT bill which remains same)	
CT saved by company:			Additional NIC	Nil
£11,040 @ 25%	2,760	Due nine months later	*Tax payable by director:*	
			Deducted at source	£2,500
			Higher rate tax (payable eight months after tax year)	1,247
				£3,747
Position of Director:				
Payment	£10,000			£10,000
Less Income Tax	3,747			3,747
Net income	6,253			6,253

In the case of the salary, **all** of the tax is payable immediately, whereas in the case of the dividend, £2,500 is payable as ACT and, if the dividend is paid right at the start of a calendar quarter, then the ACT is not payable until three and a half months later. A considerable cash flow saving. In addition the higher rate tax of £1,247 is not payable until 1 December following the tax year. A dividend should therefore be given serious consideration.

Position of the Company:

		Salary			Dividend
Profits as above		£40,000			£40,000
Less Salary & NIC		11,040	Less, Dividend		7,500
		28,960			32,500
Less, CT:					
Original	£10,000			£10,000	
Saving (above)	2,760			-	
		7,240			10,000
Profits Retained		£21,720			£22,500

The dividend route again looks attractive, the only drawback being that part of the CT bill (£2,500) has to be paid much earlier, as ACT. For those into tricky arithmetic, the difference in the retained profits above £22,500 less £21,720 = £780. This represents the additional NIC of £1,040 less CT of 25 per cent saved on this = £780!

Although in many cases it does appear attractive to pay dividends rather than salaries there are some disadvantages, notably the fact that dividends are **not** earned income and **cannot** be used as the basis for calculating final salary for pension purposes and anyone approaching pensionable age should perhaps stick to the salary route.

We can now return to the original question – should a company be used? In considering the above illustrations, it has been assumed that the business has been the owner's only source of income.

We have seen that up to income of about £50,000, the sole trader route has attractions, whereas with profits of £70,000 and above, the company looks attractive. Clearly, if an individual already has sufficient income to pay higher rate taxes, then any additional profits earned in another activity would more efficiently be earned via a company, since company profits up to £250,000 attract CT at 25 per cent as opposed to the higher personal rate of income tax of 40 per cent. The profits do have to be retained in the company, but they could be used to expand the company with a view to selling it later at a substantial gain or to provide very generous pensions for the owners via a company pension scheme. Bear in mind, however, that salaries will have to be taken sometime to justify the pension.

It should not be overlooked that a husband and wife partnership, under the independent taxation rules can be a very attractive alternative to a company up to very substantial levels of income. For example, using the illustrations shown above, the comparative figures of tax plus NIC for a husband and wife partnership would be as follows:

Income	*Sole trader*	*Company*	*Partnership (H & W)*
£50,000	£15,310	£14,929	£12,350
£70,000	23,310	19,929	19,308

The partnership enjoys the same cash flow benefit in terms of paying tax which applies to sole traders. One further possibility is to have a company with a husband and wife as directors with both taking sufficient salaries for each to utilise the basic rate band of tax. Over £56,000 could be taken without reaching the higher rate band of 40 per cent. There is, however, one major drawback in this sort of company when compared to a husband and wife partnership. Any salary paid to the spouses must be justifiable in commercial terms. That is, the salary paid must be the going rate for the work done and this is sometimes difficult to argue. Where a wife (or a husband!) arrives twice a month and tidies up the office and is paid £25,000 p.a., the Inland Revenue would simply disallow the salary as a deduction against the company's profits.

There are two final aspects of small companies which a prospective director should be aware of:

- Close Company rules
- the treatment of losses

These will be covered briefly.

Close companies

A close company is defined as one which is under the control of five or fewer participators (generally any individual with a financial interest in the company) OR is under the control of its directors however many there are. In considering shares held by any individual, any shares held by their associates (close relatives or business partners) are included. Control is broadly exercised through owning voting shares. The rules for close companies are generally anti-avoidance in nature, recognising that in such companies, the owners could be in a position to confer certain tax advantages on themselves. These could involve the granting of interest free loans with indefinite repayment dates or benefits in kind being conferred on shareholders or their associates.

Loans to participators (or their associates)

Where such loans are made, the amount is treated as a distribution by the company and the company must make a payment to the Inland Revenue equal to the current rate of ACT (currently 1/3 of the amount). Such payments are **not** deductible from the company's CT liability. The company **must** inform the Revenue of any such loans. Always seek advice before embarking on such a course – many small companies get caught out through ignorance. When the loan is repaid, the payment made is refunded but not if the loan is waived. In this case it becomes the income of the individual concerned. The rule does not apply to loans made in the ordinary course of the company's business (a loan company) or to loans not exceeding £15,000 made to full-time working directors who, with their associates, do not hold more than 5 per cent of the ordinary share capital.

Special rules apply to close investment-holding companies (CIC) but these are unlikely to apply to readers of this book.

Benefits in kind

Where benefits in kind are provided by the company to participators (or their associates) who are neither directors nor higher paid employees, then the value of such benefits is disallowed in arriving at the company's Schedule D I profit figure. An example of such a benefit could be the provision of rent-free accommodation. Benefits to directors and higher paid employees do not come within the scope of these rules since such benefits are assessed as income on the employees concerned.

Corporation tax losses

Major changes in the method of granting relief for trading losses (not capital losses) were introduced in the Finance Act 1991 (this should be borne in mind when looking at older text books). The main relieving section for company losses was Section 393 (1 – 11) and the Act repealed subsections (2 – 6), replacing them with a new Section 393A. In addition it repealed Section 394 (terminal losses) as, due to the new provisions, it is now redundant. The current version of the rules is now stated.

A **trading** loss (not a Capital loss) computed under the rules of Schedule D I – including capital allowances – sustained by a company may be relieved as follows.

The loss may be used to extinguish the **gross** income of the company (excluding FII and including gains) **before** deducting **any** charges for the **same period** as the loss.

Any **trade charges** left unrelieved, because the income is now nil, may be carried forward and set against any future trading income only (see below). These are then considered as a loss carried forward under Section 393 (1).

Any **non-trade** charges (such as charitable covenants) remaining unrelieved for the current accounting period are lost and **cannot** be carried forward.

Where any of the loss remains unrelieved, then it may be carried **back** and be set against the gross income less any trade charges of the 36 months immediately preceding the accounting period for which the loss was sustained. Later periods are relieved before earlier periods. Where the 36 months overlaps the final period being relieved, then the income to be relieved in that final year is limited to that of a period equal to the balance of the 36 months still to be used up.

Any non-trade charges, such as covenants, paid in any period where the income is reduced to nil by the loss claim, are lost and cannot be carried forward. If, after fully claiming loss relief, there remains chargeable income, then non-trade charges may be deducted.

Note that the relief obtained by carrying the loss backwards **cannot** be claimed **unless** the loss is first relieved against other income of the loss-making period. The price to be paid for carrying the loss backwards under Section 393A is that it must first be used in the loss-making period.

Any loss unrelieved after any of the above claims (or where none of the above claims have been made), may be carried forward, without time limit, and set against future **Schedule D I income only.**

Appendix – Rates of corporation tax

The following are the rates of CT and the various fractions used in computing a company's CT liability for the latest three Financial Years.

Financial Year *i.e. year ended*	*1990* *31/3/91*	*1991* *31/3/92*	*1992* *31/3/93*
Standard rate of CT	34%	33%	33%
Small company rate	25%	25%	25%
Upper Income limit	£1,000,000	£1,250,000	£1,250,000
Lower Income limit	£200,000	£250,000	£ 250,000
Taper relief fraction	1/40	1/50	1/50
ACT fraction	1/3	1/3	1/3

Note: ACT = Advance Corporation Tax

Useful references

The following Inland Revenue publications will prove helpful:

CGT 11 *Capital Gains Tax and small businesses*
CGT 13 *Capital Gains Tax – The indexation allowance for quoted shares*
CGT 14 *Capital Gains Tax – An introduction*
CGT 15 *Capital Gains Tax – A guide for married couples*
CGT 16 *Capital Gains Tax – Indexation allowance – Disposals after 5 April 1988*

7

8 Transfer of sole trader/partnership to a limited company

Income tax implications of transfer □ Basic rules of CGT □ Capital gains and business transfer □ Costs of the transfer of assets □ Illustration of a transfer of business to company

So far, this book has dealt with three different forms of business structure (sole traders, partnerships and limited companies) and in each case there have been important differences in the taxation treatment. In this chapter we will deal with the taxation implications of the decision by the owners of an existing business to form a limited company to acquire that business, the previous owners becoming the major shareholders in the new company. This decision will usually result in a potential charge to a tax not yet dealt with in this book – Capital Gains Tax (CGT).

Income tax implications of transfer

Before considering the CGT implications, it is important that any income tax implications of the decision are fully understood. Probably the most important of these is that on the transfer of the business to a company, the business of the sole trader or partnership is treated as ceasing under income tax rules. The reader is referred to Chapter 3 which contains detailed coverage of the effects of cessation and stresses the importance of the timing of the cessation in order to ensure that the maximum amount of profits 'drop out' of the assessments. Remember that ceasing just before or just after a 5th April can result in significant differences in the tax bills. Ideally, the conversion should take place when the business has reached a 'plateau' of profits sufficiently large to justify running the business as a company (see Chapter 7), and where the profits are expected to increase substantially in the next few years. If, say, profits have been at around £50,000 for the last three years, then on cessation, depending on the accounting date, at least one full year's profits will drop out. Where the profits have been level, the Revenue will not revise assessments under S. 63 (see Chapter 3).

The other possible income tax problem arising on the cessation of a business is that there could be a 'claw back' of capital allowances represented by the gains on disposal of those assets on which capital allowances had been previously claimed. In the case of the transfer of a business this claw back can be avoided where the major shareholders in the new company were the owners of the business being transferred. A claim may be made to have the assets transferred to the company at their tax written down values, with the company continuing to claim writing down allowances on these values, thus avoiding any balancing charges. This leaves capital gains tax as the main problem to deal with and before looking at the detailed provisions involved, it will be necessary to spend a little time covering some of the basic rules of CGT.

Basic rules of CGT

This tax was introduced in the 1965 Finance Act and broadly sought to tax any gains arising on the disposal of capital assets (as distinct from revenue gains such as profit). There are a number of assets excluded from the charge and the reader can find these listed in the very useful Inland Revenue Leaflet (CGT 14).

The assets with which we are concerned in the transfer of a business are almost all subject to capital gains tax (any which are not will be highlighted later in this chapter).

It can be helpful to study the computation necessary to produce a capital gain under the current regulations. This would appear as follows:

Proceeds of sale		£XXXX
Less, any costs of sale (fees, etc.)		XXXX
Net sales proceeds		XXXX
Less, The **higher** of:		
original cost of asset **or** Market value of asset at 31 March 1982	£XXXX	
(only if owned at this date)		
Plus indexation on above	XXXX	XXXX
Chargeable Gain		£XXXX

The following points will help the reader to follow the above computation:

- No gains prior to 31 March 1982 are taxable and thus the seller can use this value for any assets sold which were owned at that date. Obviously, this value cannot be used for assets acquired after 31 March 1982, these being included at their cost price plus any expenses of acquisition. Where original cost is higher than the March 1982 value, then this may be used. The idea, of course, is to get the smallest possible gain.

  Unfortunately, the taxpayer cannot use the March 1982 value where this would produce a higher loss than would arise using cost. Where the market value (MV) at 31 March 1982 produces a gain and original cost produces a loss, or vice versa, neither a gain nor a loss arises.
- The tax payer may make an irrevocable global election to have all assets valued at 31 March 1982 market value.
- The amount by which the value used has been increased as a result of inflation is allowed as a deduction from the overall gain (or as in the above layout, as an addition to the input cost). This is measured by taking the movement in the published Retail Price Index (RPI) between the date of purchase (or March 1982 if later) and the date of sale. This movement is expressed as a factor to three decimal places, and the input cost used is multiplied by this factor. Tables of these factors are published in many journals. The increase from March 1982 to May 1992 was over 70 per cent.
- Each taxpayer is entitled to an annual exemption of £5,800 which is deducted from the total gains for each year, any remaining gains being taxed at the highest rate of income tax payable by the individual dependent on the level of total income. Husbands and wives each have an annual exemption of £5,800.

Capital gains and business transfer

Why should we be concerned about capital gains in a situation where all that is happening is that an existing business is simply taking a new form and is being run by the same people? Remember that a company is a separate legal entity and what is really happening is that one taxable person (the original owner/s) is 'selling' assets consisting of a business, to another taxable person, a company. If any of these assets have an accumulated gain arising between the date they were originally acquired by the owner and the date of transfer to a company, then a capital gain will arise. This is true even where the price 'paid' by the company is in the form of shares issued to the original owners and no cash actually changes hands.

In most cases, any gain arising derives from two types of assets:

- *Goodwill.* This in many cases has no original cost where the business was started from scratch by the owner/s. In many cases it has a considerable value at the date of transfer representing all the intangible assets which a going concern possesses and which have no value placed on them in the balance sheet. The total figure represents what a willing buyer, in the open market, would pay for the business over and above the price which would be paid for the tangible assets such as premises, fittings, debtors, etc.
- *Property.* In many cases this has increased dramatically in value between the original purchase date and the date of transfer.

Much of the adviser's time is taken up with agreeing values with the Capital Taxes Office of the Revenue for these assets at the date of transfer to the company. This can sometimes be a protracted process. The gain arising as a result of the transfer to the company is the difference between the value of the shares issued (roughly equivalent to the net worth of the company after any valuations) and the original cost of the assets (or March 1982 value if higher) plus indexation.

Rollover relief

Clearly, if the person transferring the business to a limited company were required to pay capital gains tax on the gains described above, there would be some difficulty in finding the cash to pay the tax since there are generally no cash proceeds involved, (the owner receiving shares to the value of the net assets). Fortunately, S. 162 CGTA, 1992 provides total or partial relief from the need to pay any tax now. The provisions allow the taxpayer to claim a form of relief known as 'rollover relief'. This is a general relief applicable to CGT which allows the taxpayer to defer the CGT arising on the disposal of a **business asset** by deducting the assessable gain (after indexation) from the cost of a **replacement business asset**. When this latter asset is sold, the deferred gain may crystallise, since its base cost has been reduced by the rolled over gain on the first asset. On the sale of the second asset there is nothing to prevent the taxpayer claiming further rollover relief, provided this asset is also replaced by a business asset. This can be repeated as often as wished, with the accumulated gains being deferred until the taxpayer reaches sixty years of age and retires, at which time retirement relief (see Chapter 10) may be claimed and this could wipe out all the accumulated gains!

This general form of rollover relief is given under S. 152 CGTA, 1992 which sets out the detailed requirements, the most important of which are:

- The taxpayer must be carrying on a trade (or trades)
- The asset sold and its replacement must be used in the trade/s
- The proceeds of the sale of one asset must be used in acquiring the replacement (if only part of the proceeds are re-invested, the relief is restricted)
- While the asset sold and its replacement need not be identical assets, both must fall within any of the following categories: ships; aircraft; goodwill; hovercraft; fixed plant not forming part of a building; land or buildings used for a trade; spacecraft etc.; milk and potato quotas; assets used in holiday furnished lettings
- The expenditure on the replacement asset/s must take place within one year before and three years after the disposal of the original asset.

In applying the rollover principles to a situation where a company is formed to acquire the business of a sole trader or a partnership, the following points should be noted:

The chargeable gain arising can be rolled over in part or wholly provided:

- All assets (excluding cash) are transferred.
- The business is transferred as going concern
- The business is transferred wholly or partly in exchange for shares.

The gain arising is computed by deducting the original cost plus indexation of the chargeable assets being transferred, from the market value of those assets at the date of the transfer. Where the consideration is wholly in shares (which need not be ordinary shares – they may include redeemable preference shares on the redemption of which a charge to CGT will arise) then the whole of the gain may be rolled over. Where the transfer is partly for shares and partly for cash (or loans or loan stock), then the following proportion only of the overall gain may be deferred:

$$\text{Overall gain} \times \frac{\text{Value of shares}}{\text{Value of total consideration}}$$

(See illustration at the end of the chapter.)

Where it has been decided not to transfer all of the assets to the company, or where some of them consist of investments, then these could be transferred to a spouse some time before incorporation (no CGT on the transfer). The annual exemption and any unrelieved capital losses should be kept in mind in deciding which of the assets should be retained.

A major disadvantage of using S. 162 is that all the assets (apart from cash) of the business must be transferred to obtain rollover relief. It may be the case that the owner of the business wishes to keep the premises in his own name, in which case the CGT arising on the gains on the assets which are being transferred would become payable and could not be deferred under S. 162. An alternative approach is possible, utilising the holdover relief on gifts under S. 165 CGTA, 1992, which avoids the need to transfer all the assets. The use of S. 165 is fairly complex and is beyond the scope of this book. Where a trader feels its use is appropriate – i.e. he wishes to retain an asset such as property – expert advice should be sought. A major advantage of using S. 162 is that the assets are transferred to the company at market value and indexation will be calculated on this figure when the **company** sells the assets. (The rollover reduces the value of the shares in the hands of the **individuals** and their indexation is calculated on this reduced value when they come to sell the shares.

Retirement relief

On incorporation care should be taken to ensure that none of the shareholders in the new company is deprived of potential retirement relief. The absolute minimum shareholding required to be in a position to qualify for retirement relief is 5 per cent (provided such a shareholder is a member of a 'family company' – see Chapter 10). For those not in such a company the minimum shareholding is 25 per cent.

In a case where a husband and wife are in partnership with only the husband (or wife) working full-time in the business, then both would qualify for retirement relief (see Chapter 10).

In a company situation, only the full-time working directors would qualify.

Costs of the transfer of the assets

A final point which must not be overlooked is that there will be unavoidable costs involved on the transfer of the assets. These will consist mainly of legal and accounting fees and it must not be forgotten that stamp duty and capital duty may be payable. These latter costs can be substantial and advice should be sought on methods of mitigating them. For instance, it may be more efficient for the existing owner to collect outstanding trading debts at the date of transfer rather than having them transferred to the new company.

Illustration of a transfer of business to company

Mr Engelbert McTavish, aged 52, transfers the assets and liabilities of his business to Haggis Ltd on 1 January 1993 in exchange for:

- 10,000 Ordinary shares of £1 each
- 5,000 Preference shares of £1 each
- £9,000 in cash

The gain on the transfer was £56,000 being the market value of the net assets of £74,000 less the original cost and indexation allowance amounting to £18,000.

The MV of the shares at the date of transfer was:

- Ordinary shares £5
- Preference shares £3

Mr McTavish sells his ordinary shares on 1 January 1995 for £70,000.

Assuming rollover relief is claimed on the transfer, compute the chargeable gain before indexation.

Solution

Portion of the overall gain which may be rolled over:

$$£56{,}000 \times \frac{\text{Value of shares received}}{\text{Total consideration}}$$

$$£56{,}000 \times \frac{£50{,}000 + £15{,}000}{£50{,}000 + £15{,}000 + £9{,}000}$$

$$= £49{,}189$$

The balance of the gain – £56,000 – £49,189 = £6,811 – which would be chargeable to capital gains tax. If Mr McTavish had no other gains in the tax year, he could use his annual exemption of £5,800, reducing the taxable gain to £1,011. It is sometimes possible to structure the consideration so that the chargeable gain is exactly £5,800 and wiped out by the exemption.

The deferred gain of £49,189 is apportioned between the ordinary shares and the preference shares, so that the reduced base cost of each holding would be:

Ordinary shares – MV at date of transfer		£50,000
Less, gain rolled over	$£49{,}189 \times \frac{£50{,}000}{£65{,}000} =$	37,838
Base cost of ordinary shares for CGT		£12,162

The preference shares would be dealt with similarly:

MV at date of transfer	£15,000
Less gain rolled over (£49,189 – 37,838 above)	11,351
	£ 3,649

When the ordinary shares are sold on 1 January 1995 the chargeable gain will be:

Proceeds	£70,000
Less, base cost as above	12,162
Gain before indexation	£57,838

This gain would be reduced by the indexation allowance for the period January 1993 to January 1995.

It would appear that Mr McTavish has made a disastrous blunder by selling his shares when he is aged 54 since he will not qualify for retirement relief (which is given at age 55). Had he waited until he was 55, the above gain would have been totally extinguished by retirement relief. As it stands, his tax bill could be around £20,000!

---

9 The taxation of employees

Employing staff □ Setting up a system □ Defining 'pay' and when it is made □ PAYE □ Benefits in kind to certain directors and higher paid employees □ Defining some benefits in kind □ Employee/self-employed □ Help in the processes of employee taxation □ Appendix 1 – Rates of NIC 1992/93

So far this book has dealt with the taxation position of the owners of a business whether they are sole traders, partners or directors of a company owned by them. In the latter case, it was pointed out that directors were in fact employees of the company and therefore subject to the PAYE system (pay as you earn). Whatever the status of the owners, it was always **their** tax which was discussed.

In this chapter we will be looking at a different aspect of taxation – the way in which employers, whatever the structure of their business, become involved in the taxation (and national insurance contributions – NIC) of their employees (who are taxed under the rules of Schedule E). This will be dealt with under two main areas:

- the tax arrangements for employees who are **not** directors (or employees with total emoluments of at least £8,500);
- the special taxation rules applicable to **most** directors and other employees with total emoluments of at least £8,500 who are in receipt of non-cash benefits from the company (e.g. the use of motor cars).

The first point to note is that considerable work is involved in complying with the statutory duties imposed on all employers for the operation of the PAYE system. The employer becomes an unpaid tax collector! It is even more important to appreciate that the penalties involved for failing to comply with the system can be very severe. You should avoid becoming involved in a PAYE investigation. The knock-on effect of such an investigation should be borne in mind – if the investigation reveals serious breaches of the system, then the future accounts of the business may, perhaps, lack credibility in the eyes of the Inspector of Taxes!

There comes a time in the development of most small businesses when it becomes necessary to take on help in the form of either part-time or full-time workers. It may be that some readers have already done this on a casual basis and have done nothing officially about it and are possibly terrified at what they have read above! These persons and those about to take on staff for the first time should, if they pay careful attention to what follows, be able to stay out of trouble.

It is important to grasp that the onus is wholly on the employer to deduct the correct tax (and NIC) from the appropriate employees and to pay it over to the tax authorities at the correct time. An employer who fails to do so can be asked to account for all the tax and NIC not deducted *plus* interest and penalties. If tax has not been deducted from say, three employees earning £8,000 p.a. each for say three years, then the final bill for the employer could be frightening!

So, what should be done if staff are taken on for the first time?

Employing staff

The first thing to do **before** taking on anyone is to advise the tax district dealing with employers in your district (contact the employers unit) that you intend taking staff on (it is possible that they have contacted you earlier regarding the operation of PAYE when they became aware of the business). The tax office will send you a standard Employer's pack (P4) containing all the tables and documentation required to operate the system. This contains extremely clear and well written instructions on the basic aspects of PAYE and NIC and you should familiarise yourself with the main features of the systems which are set out in the employers' *Guides* (one for PAYE and one for NIC). There are also available guides to Statutory Sick Pay (SSP) and Statutory Maternity Pay (SMP). The Employer's pack (P4) also contains all the forms referred to below.

The first problem you have to deal with is setting the system up and becoming clear on what you have to do in respect of your first new employee.

Setting up a system

For most employees, an employer is required to prepare a 'deductions working sheet', a specimen copy of which, in poster style, is included in the pack. This is extremely clear and easy to follow. An easy to follow guide on the procedure to adopt for new employees is contained on Form P 8 (and in paragraph D 43 of the *Employer's Guide*, two flow charts at Table A and Table B explain very clearly the employer's duties). The particular procedure to be used depends on whether the new employee produces a Form P 45 – lots of people are unfortunately all too familiar with this form!

The following is a brief summary of the processes:

Where the employee produces a P 45

- Prepare a deduction sheet (P 11) for the employee following the instructions on Form P 8. This must be done even where the employee's wage will be below the tax threshold (currently £66.50 per week or £288 per month) and the NIC threshold (currently £54 per week or £234 per month). This can be important when dealing with part-time employees.
- Complete and send part 3 of the form to the Revenue and retain part 2 carefully.
- Using the Free Pay table and the Taxable Pay tables as instructed in Form P 8, calculate the weekly or monthly tax payable (or refundable). Using the appropriate NIC tables calculate the employee's and employer's NIC payable. The weekly (or monthly) figures for pay, tax and NIC must be entered on the deduction sheet. **Note** carefully that where a refund of over £200 appears to be due on the employee's first pay day, then you must apply to the Revenue (P 47) for permission to make the refund and *must not do so until* the Revenue send you Form P 48. This is to prevent abuse of the system.
- Remit to the Revenue all tax and NIC (including employer's NIC) for all employees for the period up to the 5th of each month, no later than the 19th of that month. A payment book with payslips is provided.

9

Where the employee does not produce a P 45

The procedure depends on whether the employee is a school or college leaver for whom this is their first job or simply someone who has either lost their P 45 or not been given one by their former employer.

Where the employee is in the first category (and certifies that this is so on Form P 46) and the weekly pay is below both the tax

and NIC levels, then it is only necessary to keep a note of their name and address and the amount paid. No deduction sheet need be kept. Where their pay is above the NIC threshold, then a deduction sheet must be kept recording the NIC details. Form P 46 should be retained by the employer for three years.

Where the employee is in this category and will be paid at a rate **above** the tax threshold, then the single person's code number should be used (currently 344 L) and tax calculated on a cumulative basis as instructed in P 8. Form P 46 should be filled in and sent to the Inland Revenue straight away.

Where any other employee starts and fails to produce a P 45, then provided they certify on Form P 46 that this is their only/main employment, and their pay is below the thresholds, the treatment is exactly as described for school/college leavers above.

Where such employees will be paid more than the tax threshold, then special rules apply. The employee is given the Emergency code (currently 344 L) which is applied on a 'week (or Month) 1 basis' and tax calculated on a non-cumulative basis as instructed in P 8.

All tax and NIC collected from such staff is remitted, together with the employer's NIC, as described above.

What happens when an employee leaves?

In all cases the employer is required to complete Form P 45 and send part 1 to the Revenue and give parts 2 and 3 to the employee. The procedure for filling in the form is described in P 8 (again!) and paragraphs D 46–47 of the *Employer's Guide* (P 7) should be read by those doing this for the first time.

What happens at the end of the tax year?

You will be left in no doubt as to your duties at this time as the Revenue will inundate you with various forms and most helpful guides as to how these should be completed.

Basically what you have to do is summarise – on Form P 35 – all the tax and NIC for each employee for the year, add it up and reconcile it with the amounts you have remitted to the Revenue during the year. If it squares exactly the first time you try it – give yourself a pat on the back!

You are also required to complete, for each employee, Form P 14. This form is in three parts, the first two parts being sent to the tax office with Form P 35. The third part is the employee's proof of pay, tax and NIC for the year (called a P 60) and should be given to each employee on the first pay day after 5th April each year. It is a most important document and failure to produce it may result in a delay in obtaining benefits such as unemployment benefit.

The literature sent to you shortly before the year end includes an enlarged version of Form P 14 showing clearly how each section is to be completed.

This has been a brief summary of the operation of the system and more information can be obtained by studying the employer's guide. If you cannot resolve a particular problem, do not hesitate to contact your local tax office. They are extremely helpful and can usually sort out your difficulties very quickly.

Defining 'pay' and when it is made

A common difficulty which employers encounter is what to include on the deduction working sheet as 'pay'. So far this chapter has assumed that employees are paid only straightforward wages or salaries which clearly should be entered. If a payment described as something other than wages is made, it generally has to be included on the deduction sheet as pay. Paragraph B 9 of the *Guide* lists these payments and the following are some of the more commonly encountered:

9

- commission
- pensions
- honoraria
- holiday pay
- Statutory Sick Pay
- Statutory Maternity Pay
- travelling time
- cash payments for meals
- certain lump sums paid on leaving employment (see Paragraph F 73).

There are other, more obscure items on the list which should be studied carefully **before** making the payment. If in doubt, ring the tax office.

Directors' remuneration

In the case of directors who are often paid on a different basis from other employees (they are voted bonuses or allowed to draw advances of salary or bonuses) there are special new rules which were introduced in the Finance Act 1989. These are now summarised.

Payment of remuneration is regarded as being made (and therefore included on the deduction sheet) on the **earliest** of the following dates:

- when the payment is actually made
- when the director becomes **entitled** to be paid (although not actually paid)
- when the amount is credited to the director in the company accounts or records (even if he cannot draw on it at that point).

There is one remaining problem in this area and that is how to establish when remuneration is 'determined' and thus treated as paid and entered on the deduction sheet. Where remuneration has not already been paid (or treated as paid) under the above three rules, it is to be treated as paid when **voted** at the companies AGM and PAYE should be operated at that date. If the remuneration is determined before the AGM (say at a directors' or shareholders' meeting) then the effective date for PAYE purposes is the date of determination.

Finally if the remuneration is determined for a company's accounting period **before** that period ends, then the effective date is taken as the date when the period **actually ends**.

Ex gratia payments to directors

Directors of small companies are often in a position to do themselves an enormous favour when retiring from office by receiving a large lump sum on leaving office (this in large companies always attracts press coverage). While the first £30,000 of any *ex gratia* payment is free of tax in the hands of the recipient, great care should be taken to establish that the **Revenue agree** that the payment is indeed *ex gratia*. Paragraph F 73 of the *Guide* should be studied most carefully and if in any doubt, always check with the tax office **before** making the payment. It is, of course, always open to the company to challenge the Revenue's opinion, and expert advice should be sought.

Whether the payment made, even if it is tax free in the hands of the retiring director, will be allowed as a deduction in arriving at the company's taxable profits is another story and maybe more expert advice will be required!

PAYE

Throughout this chapter reference has been made to employee's 'code numbers' and to absolute beginners this might be causing some puzzlement. A brief explanation should clear up any confusion.

A PAYE code number allows an employer to give the correct weekly or monthly allowances to each employee on a cumulative basis. The idea is to spread the appropriate allowances evenly over the tax year. For example, the personal allowance is currently £3,445 and this has to be spread evenly over the tax year. The code number is derived by omitting the last figure and thus the code number would be 344. When this code is looked up in the free pay tables it shows the accumulated allowance up to date. If Week 26 was involved, the total allowances to date would be approximately one half of £3,445. The tables actually give a slightly higher figure than £3,445 over the whole year. A married man's allowance would be £3,445 plus the married couple's allowance of £1,720 = £5,165, giving a code number of 516. Where the taxpayer is not married, the code number will have a suffix 'L', and if married 'H' and if elderly 'P' or 'V'.

Where the taxpayer is entitled to other allowances e.g. expenses, then the code number will be higher than the above figures. Alternatively, where the taxpayer has other income which has not been taxed, the Revenue may deduct this from the allowances due (thus collecting the tax on it) and the code number will be lower than the basic allowances.

Where the code has a suffix of L, H, P or V, this allows budget changes to be put into effect quickly by simply increasing them by the increases in personal allowances announced in the budget.

Code numbers with any other prefix (or suffix) cannot be amended in this way and special rules apply. A description of these other codes and their implications are again explained in P 8 with a fuller coverage given in paragraph B 12 of the *Employer's Guide*.

SSP, SMP and NIC

The other areas for which an employer can become responsible are Statutory Sick Pay (SSP) and Statutory Maternity Pay (SMP). It is not proposed to deal with the detailed rules in this book (about tax!). Just about all an employer needs to know about these areas is clearly spelt out in the DSS *Quick Guide to the NIC, SSP and SMP* (NI 268). Very briefly, the idea in each of these systems is that the employer pays SSP or SMP directly to the employee (at prescribed rates) and recovers this money by deducting it (plus any NIC paid on it) from future payments of PAYE and NIC to the Revenue.

Finally, before leaving this area, it should be noted that the method of calculating NIC for company directors can differ from that applicable to other employees. Reference should be made to NI Leaflet 35 plus appropriate supplements.

The PAYE, SSP and SMP rules apply to **all** employees (whether they are directors or not) although the method of taxing certain payments (generally bonuses) made to directors requires special consideration as we have seen.

The various rates of NIC for employees and employers are shown in the appendix to this chapter and it should be noted that where the employer runs an approved pension scheme for employees, then both contribution figures are at the lower 'contracted out' rates. The table also reveals that while a 'ceiling' exists for employees' contributions (currently a wage of £405 per week), no such limit applies to employers' contributions. It costs the employer 10.4 per cent of **all** wages where the wage is over £190 per week. Compare this with the NIC contributions of the self-employed (see examples in Chapter 7).

This leads nicely into a discussion on non-cash payments to directors (and other higher paid employees) since such benefits do not normally attract NIC!

Benefits in kind to certain directors and higher paid employees

There is a considerable amount of legislation devoted to this area and it can sometimes be difficult to interpret. This complexity can often lead to inadvertent non-compliance with the legislation and it is wise to seek advice when in doubt. All employers should receive a copy of the Revenue booklet 480 dealing with expenses and benefits for 'directors and certain employees'. This should be studied together with Paragraph E 57 of the *Employer's Guide*. The legislation broadly seeks to identify those benefits, either in the form of assets provided for employees, or in the form of expense payments made to the employees, which are taxable and those which are not. It also covers the treatment of certain expenses paid by employees in the course of their employment.

The first problem to solve is – which employees are affected by these benefit rules?

There are two groups of employees subject to the rules

- ALL employees, whether directors or not, whose total remuneration, including all potentially assessable benefits, and after deducting certain expenses, is £8,500 or more.
- ALL directors, whatever their remuneration, other than 'full-time working directors'. These latter persons are broadly directors who:

  (a) work full time for the company
  (b) together with their associates own no more than 5 per cent of the shares
  (c) have remuneration (defined above) of less than £8,500.

The figure of £8,500 can hardly be regarded, at present salary levels, as describing an employee as 'higher paid'! There is a reason for this low figure which has remained unchanged for several years. When the figure was first introduced, it did represent a high salary, and thus only a relatively small number of employees were assessed on benefits. All other employees could receive a whole range of benefits, such as motor cars, tax free. This was regarded as an unfair advantage, and the way in which the government have brought many more employees into the benefits net is to leave the figure unchanged and let general rises in wages do the rest.

Defining some benefits in kind

Benefits in kind fall broadly into three categories:

- those which are tax free
- those which are taxable in the hands of all employees

- those which are taxable only in the hands of directors and higher paid employees.

It is not proposed to list every possible benefit and following are examples of some common items included in each of the above categories.

Tax free benefits

- meals provided by the employer on the business premises (provided available to **all** employees)
- reasonable removal expenses on relocation of employment
- pension and life insurance contributions to approved schemes by employer.

Taxable on all employees

- travel tickets for non-business purposes (home to work)
- certain living accommodation (not if job requires it)
- vouchers for cash, goods or services (or purchases by company credit card)

Taxable only in the hands of directors and employees earning at least £8,500 p.a.

(By implication – tax free in the hands of all other employees)

- use of motor cars
- use of other assets
- loans at low rates of interest
- medical insurance

While such benefits are taxable, their use as an alternative to larger salaries has considerable advantages both from the employee's and the employer's points of view. One is the fact that the method of quantifying some benefits is extremely favourable but the main advantage is that very few benefits attract NIC and given that the employer's NIC is 10.4 per cent of earnings, then substantial savings can be achieved by using benefits.

Motor cars and other assets provided by an employer are probably the most common form of benefits (particularly for directors of small companies – note that the benefits system can apply to employees of sole traders or partnerships but not to the owners themselves). It will be helpful to study just how the value of the benefit is calculated. From 1992 onwards, employers must pay NIC at 10.4 per cent on the amount of car benefits assessed on all employees.

Motor cars

Where a car is provided, the employee is assessed to tax on a figure obtained from a table published by the Revenue reproduced below showing the current values:

1992–93	**Age of car at end of year of assessment**	
	Under 4 years	*4 years or more*
	£	£
Original market value up to £19,250		
1,400cc or less	2,140	1,460
1,401cc–2,000cc	2,770	1,880
More than 2,000cc	4,440	2,980
Original market value more than £19,500		
More than £19,250 but not more than £29,000	5,750	3,870
More than £29,000	9,300	6,170

Where a motor car has no cylinder capacity the table values depend on the cost of the car.

Where the employee is required to make a contribution towards the running costs of the car (and makes the contribution), then the above figures are reduced by such contribution (which may entirely eliminate the benefit). The figures are also varied as follows:

- where the business mileage is not more than 2,500 in the tax year or where a second car is provided, the figures are increased by 50 per cent
- where the business mileage is at least 18,000 in the year, the figures are reduced by 50 per cent (a longish business trip near the end of the year could be helpful!)
- where the car was unavailable for more than 30 consecutive days, the scale figures (and mileage figures) are reduced proportionately

A 'pooled car' i.e. broadly for general use by different employees, does not give rise to taxable benefits.

In addition to the above, where a car is provided to an employee and the employer meets **any** part of the employee's private fuel costs, then an additional benefit is assessed, the figure being obtained from the table shown below:

1992/93 *Cylinder capacity*	*Cash equivalent* £
1,400cc or less	500
1,401cc–2,000cc	630
More than 2,000cc	940
Diesel *Cylinder capacity*	
1,400cc or less	460
1,401cc–2,000cc	460
More than 2,000cc	590

In order to escape this charge, an employee must be required to make payment for **all** private fuel provided (contributions of less than all are ignored). The figures are reduced by 50 per cent where the business mileage is at least 18,000 but **not** increased if this figure is 2,500 or less, or if a second car is provided.

Where only a small amount of private fuel is used – worth say £100 – it is in the employee's interest to pay for it instead of having to pay tax on, say £600 at 25 per cent (or 40 per cent).

Car and fuel benefits – illustration

Mr I. Reader is the sales director of a large publishing company. At 6 April 1992 Mr Reader had the sole use of a Vauxhall Carlton car – cubic capacity 2,200cc – which had cost £18,000 when first purchased by the company in 1991. On 6 July 1992, this was replaced with a Mercedes car costing £27,000 (2,600cc) which was used by him for the rest of the tax year. Up to 5 July, his business mileage was 6,000 and from 6 July till 5 April 1993, it was 15,000. He was provided with all of his private fuel.

His wife, who did not work for the company, was provided with a Vauxhall Cavalier car costing £11,000 in 1990 – cubic capacity 1,600cc – for the whole of the tax year 1992/93. Her husband paid the annual insurance premium of £280 and paid £260 for one half of her private petrol for the year.

Compute the benefit assessable on Mr Reader for the tax year 1992/93.

Car benefit

Carlton	6/4/92–5/7/92 (3 months): 3/12 × £4,440 =		£1,110	
Mercedes	6/7/92–5/4/93 (9 months): 9/12 × £5,750 =		£4,312	
			5,422	
Less 50% (mileage over 18,000 in year):			2,711	
			£2,711	
Cavalier –	scale figure	£2,770		
	plus 50% (second car)	1,385		
		£4,155		
	Less contribution	280		
			3,875	
Total car benefit				£6,586

Fuel benefit

Carlton/Mercedes: £940 × 50% (mileage over 18,000)	£ 470	
Cavalier (no reduction for contribution)	630	
		£1,100
Total benefits assessable on Mr Reader		£7,686

Note: Had Mr Reader paid for **all** of his wife's private fuel (i.e. £520), there would have been no fuel benefit assessed on the Cavalier.

He is being taxed on £630 @ 40% =	£252
And he has paid a contribution of	260
Total cost to him	512

Had he paid **all** the fuel, he would have had no assessment but would have paid out £520 – £8 worse off.

It will be noted that the employee is getting a very good bargain. In addition, the employer can claim **full** capital allowances WDA of 25 per cent. For instance, where a new two litre car (plus all running costs) is provided for an employee paying tax at 25 per cent, the only cost to the employee is additional tax of:

£2,770 @ 25% = £692.50

Rather less than it would cost if privately owned! The fuel benefit would cost an additional:

£630 @ 25% = £157.50

A final point on motor cars

Sometimes employees are paid a mileage allowance by their employer for using their own car for business purposes. Provided this does no more than cover the costs of the employee, there will be no assessment to tax or NIC on the employee. A table of the maximum rates acceptable to the Revenue is published from time to time. It is important to agree the rate with the Revenue before paying it.

Other assets

Employees who provide their own car for business purposes may claim as a deduction capital allowances and loan interest on loans used to purchase the car (both amounts being restricted to the business use portion). Where assets (other than cars or living accommodation) are provided for directors or higher paid empoyees, the annual taxable amount is taken as 20 per cent of the market value of the asset when first provided to the employee. Where the employer rents the asset and the annual rental is higher than 20 per cent of its MV, then the benefit is the rent paid.

The range of assets which a company can provide for employees is limited only by the imagination of the employer! Chapter 4 of the Revenue booklet 480 actually gives suggestions – TV sets and furniture – but there is no reason why it should not include the director's good suits or their scuba diving equipment! It is usually more efficient for the company to provide the asset rather than give the director additional salary to enable him to purchase the item.

If, for example, the director was keen on a complete video system costing £3,000, the two possibilities are:

1. If the director were a higher rate taxpayer he would require additional salary of £5,000 (less 40 per cent = £3,000). He would

not pay any additional NIC (over limit) but the company would have to pay employer's NIC of 10.4 per cent on £5,000 = £520. The total cash outflow for the company would be £5,520. This amount would be deductible from profits and eventually save corporation tax – a longer term cash saving.

2. If the company buys the system and provides it for the director the cash outflow is £3,000 (no NIC) and the director will pay tax each year on 20 per cent of £3,000 = £600 at 40 per cent = £240.

The one other benefit which it might be helpful to look at is the provision of cheap loans. The purpose of the legislation is to tax the benefit obtained by an employee who receives a loan from his employer at a rate less than the commercial rate applying to other loans (the Revenue from time to time announce this rate). There is no benefit where the interest would qualify for tax relief – e.g. loans up to £30,000 on sole residence, where the borrower is a basic rate taxpayer.

Where the actual interest paid in any year falls short of the interest which would be paid if the commercial rate applied by £300 or less then no assessable benefit arises. If the difference is £301, then the **full** £301 is assessed! If possible, the shortfall should clearly be kept to a maximum of £300 per year.

Reporting to the Revenue

The employer has a duty to report to the Revenue the various benefits provided to all employees. This is done, for directors and higher paid employees, on Form P 11D, one for each person in receipt of benefits or expense payments. These forms are sent to each employer shortly before the end of each tax year together with a very comprehensive instruction sheet (P 11D (*Guide*)). In certain cases, where the only expense payments made to an employee consisted of those types of expenses which the employee would be allowed to deduct in arriving at his taxable income e.g. a reimbursement of allowable travel expenses – then a dispensation from returning such items can be obtained. This must be **applied for** to the Revenue.

A final question arises – how are these benefits taxed?

Most commonly the Revenue will show the amounts as deductions from the allowances used in arriving at the employee's code number, thus collecting the tax through the PAYE system. This explains why some company directors have very small code numbers! The benefits almost (or totally) extinguish the allowances. The taxpayer is entitled, at the end of each tax year, to ask the Revenue to issue an assessment showing the full tax position.

Employee/self-employed

Throughout this chapter it has been assumed that everyone who works for a business is automatically classed as an 'employee'. In practice it is not always so clear cut. Many employers will, when they offer someone a position (particularly where commission is the form of payment), be informed by that person that they are 'self-employed' and therefore not subject to PAYE or NIC. This has attractions for the employer too – no need for PAYE or NIC records and most attractive of all, **no** employer's NIC. In such circumstances – **beware**!

However attractive it might be to engage someone on this basis, an employer must be absolutely sure that the person being 'taken on' is indeed **entitled** to be classed as self-employed. It is not enough simply to have the person sign a piece of paper saying he will be responsible for his own tax and NIC. The onus is on the employer to apply PAYE and NIC to all employees and if there is **any doubt** concerning the status of the new recruit – treat him as an **employee**. If a dispute arises, contact the tax office and/or seek professional advice. Sometimes a carefully worded contract or agreement may establish the person as 'self-employed', but it may not be conclusive evidence of such status. Remember the employer has to pay the tax and NIC which he has failed to deduct!

Help with the processes of employee taxation

As mentioned at the start of this chapter, the employer becomes an unpaid tax collector for the Revenue and the work involved in running the PAYE, NIC, SSP and SMP systems can be difficult, costly and time consuming. Much of the 'hassle' can be removed where the business is already using, or has access to, any modestly priced personal computer. An extremely efficient and easy to operate payroll system can be purchased for under £100 and this will take care of everything – payslips; employee records; monthly payments to the Revenue and **all** of the end of the year routines and documentation. It will prove an excellent investment. Further information can be obtained from the Inland Revenue publication *Computerised Payroll* (IR 70). Note that the prices suggested for the hardware and software in this booklet should not scare you off! For small businesses with less than fifty employees the figures could be reduced by a factor of ten!

Other useful references

The following Inland Revenue publications will prove helpful:

IR 53	*Thinking of taking someone on?*
IR 56/NI 139	*Employed or self-employed?*
IR 57	*Thinking of working for yourself?*
IR 69	*Expenses – Form P 11D*
IR 71	*PAYE – inspection of employer's records*
IR 24	*Class 4 National Insurance Contributions*
P 7	*Employer's Guide to PAYE*
IR 34	*Income Tax – Pay as you earn*
480	*Notes on expense payments and benefits for directors and certain employees*

Appendix – Rates of National Insurance Contributions 1992/93

Class 1 – Employed persons

Rates payable on **all** earnings shown

Contracted in (to State system)

Weekly pay – £	*Employer*	*Employee*
0–53.99	Nil	Nil
54–89.99	4.6%	2% first £54 – 9% on rest
90–134.99	6.6%	same
135–189.99	8.6%	same
190–405	10.4%	same
over 405	10.4%	Maximum payment £32.67 (nil on wages over £405)

Contracted out (of State system)

Weekly pay – £	*Employer*	*Employee*
0–53.99	Nil	Nil
54–89.99	4.6% first £54 – 0.8% on rest	2% first £54 – 7% on rest
90–134.99	6.6% first £54 – 2.8% on rest	same
135–189.99	8.6% first £54 – 4.8% on rest	same
190–405	10.4% first £54 – 6.6% on rest	same
over 405	10.4% first £54 and earnings over £405 – 6.6% on rest	Maximum payment £25.65 (nil on wages over £405)

Self-employed

Class 2

Flat rate £5.35 per week (small earnings exemption limit £3,030 p.a.)

Class 4

6.3% of profits between £6,120 and £21,060 (maximum for year £941) (paid with Schedule D I tax in two instalments 1 January/1 July) One half of Class 4 contributions is allowed as a deduction against tax.

10 Disposing of the business

Retirement relief □ Family company □ Apportionment of gains □ Impact of taxation on business disposal □ Case study

A very common question asked by those running businesses is, 'What happens when the business is sold?' It is important that this question is addressed at an early stage in the business's life since planning for the sale and eventual retirement is vital if advantage is to be taken of any reliefs on offer.

Those fortunate people who retire from business in the certain knowledge that they will have no financial problems for the rest of their life have either been members of a good pension scheme or have run a successful business for most of their life and on the occasion of their retirement, they dispose of the business making a substantial gain. This chapter is concerned with this latter group.

Retirement relief

In many cases individuals running a business have started it from scratch and for many years have put in long hours turning it into a successful enterprise which will be an attractive acquisition for other businesses. During their business life these individuals have paid taxation on their annual profits and the value of their business could be regarded as their after-tax savings. It is, therefore, appropriate that when they reach retirement age and sell their business they should be able to 'cash in' their savings without being hit with a substantial capital gains tax bill. The relief available in these circumstances is known as **Retirement relief** and this chapter will deal with the detailed provisions contained in Section 163 CGTA, 1992. While it is often the case that the individuals are actually selling their business, or their interest in a business, it is also likely they are not actually selling the business but passing it on to their children or other relatives by means of a gift.

In these circumstances, retirement relief is also available, but in addition there will possibly be Inheritance Tax implications which will be discussed later in this chapter.

Eligibility for retirement relief

The present rules apply to disposals made on or after 6 April 1985. Broadly the provisions grant relief from CGT up to a maximum figure, on material disposal of business assets by an eligible person. The detailed conditions for obtaining relief are:

- The taxpayer has attained the age of fifty five years (NB he does not need to **retire** or **retires** at a younger age through ill health). The Revenue will require medical evidence of this.
- The taxpayer disposes of the whole or a part of a business or disposes of shares or securities in a family company (see later). The provisions extend to personally owned assets used in a business and to assets provided by an employee for the purpose of his job. Where a business has ceased trading, then disposals of assets within 12 months thereafter will also attract relief, provided they were used for the trade at the date of cessation.
- Throughout the period of at least one year ending on the date of the disposal the relevant qualification requirements were fulfilled. A most important point! It is therefore **vital** that the taxpayer satisfies **all** the conditions for the relief **at the date of retirement** – otherwise **no** relief will be available. This point is especially important when dealing with family companies as we shall see.

Note

Although this indicates that the person retiring has to be 55 years of age in order to qualify for the relief (or if retiring earlier be able to provide evidence of ill health), a fairly common situation arises where a person, in good health, sells a business (which he has run for about eight years) at the age of, say 52, and retires. Clearly, no retirement relief is available. If however, after one year (at the age of 53) he starts another business which he runs for three years until he is 56 and once more retires, selling the business at a gain, retirement relief will be available against the gain arising on the second disposal. In calculating the qualifying period, part of the previous period when he ran the first business may be taken into account. In this case nine years relief would be given.

Amount of the relief

The maximum relief available to a qualifying person is, currently, the first £150,000 of the gains plus one half of the gains between £150,000 and £600,000. Full relief will be available only where the relevant conditions have been satisfied throughout the **ten** years prior to the disposal.

Where less than ten years is involved, the relief is scaled down pro rata. Thus where a person has been in a qualifying position for only eight years then the maximum relief available will be 8/10 of £150,000 = £120,000 plus one half of the balance of the gains over £120,000 up to a maximum of £480,000 (i.e. 8/10 × £600,000). Note that **all** gains over £600,000 (or £480,000 in this example) are fully taxable and that a husband and wife are **both** entitled to the maximum figures **each** so that a husband and wife in an equal partnership could obtain full relief on the first £300,000 of gains.

Illustration

Mr Al Dunn, aged 57, sold his business on 30 June 1993, realising a gain of £440,000. He had originally acquired the business on 1 January 1986. All of the assets were business assets (see later)

Chargeable gain			£440,000
Less retirement relief (7½ years)			
7½/10 × £150,000		£112,500	
Calculation of one half additional relief:			
Excess of gains over £112,500	– £327,500		
(£440,000 – 112,500)			
Maximum on which one half given			
7½/10 × £450,000	£337,500		
Therefore relief ½ × £327,500		163,750	
			£276,250
Gain assessed (subject to annual exemption)			£163,750

Family company

Where shares in a 'family company' are being sold or gifted on retirement, great care must be taken to ensure that those persons likely to claim retirement relief satisfy **all** the conditions **at the date of retirement**.

An individual is regarded as being part of a family company where:

---

1. The individual has not less than 25 per cent of the voting rights in his own name.

OR

2. Has not less than five per cent of the voting rights and he and his family (spouse, and relatives such as antecedents, children, grandchildren, brothers and sisters but not uncles, cousins or nephews, etc.) hold more than 50 per cent of the voting rights. It is most important to ensure nobody is precluded from the relief as a result of either being, say, one share short of the 25 per cent or five per cent requirement.

A common mistake made by small companies is to allow the shares to be owned by relatives who **do not count** as family (nephews, etc.) with the result that while an individual retiring owns, say 20 per cent, the 'family' as defined for these purposes, fail to control more than 50 per cent. Such an individual gets **no** retirement relief, despite the fact that he has been involved in the business for 20 years.

Illustration

Mr McGone, aged 61, retires from his business when the various shareholdings were:

	Situation A	*Situation B*
Mr McGone	20%	24%
Mrs McGone	20%	20%
His son	10%	6%
His daughter	5%	–
Nephews and nieces	45%	50%

In situation A, Mr McGone would qualify for retirement relief since his 'family' (for CGT purposes) own **more** than 50 per cent of the shares. In situation B, he would not qualify since he does not personally own 25 per cent and his 'family' does not own **more** than 50 per cent.

In qualifying cases the shares must also be held for **ten** years to obtain maximum relief and at least **one** year (ending with the date of retirement) to obtain 10 per cent of the relief. Where a business has been incorporated, then the aggregate period of owning the business before incorporation and owning any shares subsequently issued is taken.

To qualify for the relief, the individual must be a full-time working director throughout the period of owning the shares.

Apportionment of gains

Where a business which is not a company is being sold on retirement, it is possible to identify the individual gains arising on **each** asset being sold. This makes the calculation of the relief fairly straightforward since only certain assets can attract retirement relief. These assets consist of those which are used in the trade such as goodwill, property, certain plant and machinery (but not debtors, stock or cash). These assets are described as *chargeable business assets*. Other assets which the business owns, such as investments, which can also give rise to a chargeable gain, are regarded as non-business assets and the gain arising is fully taxable and cannot attract retirement relief.

A problem arises where an individual qualifies for retirement relief by virtue of selling (or gifting) shares in a family company, since the individual is not selling identifiable assets in a business. What is being sold is a block of shares!

In such a case it is necessary to compute the overall gain on the shares which is arrived at by taking the proceeds (or MV in the case of a gift) and subtracting from this the original cost (or MV at 31 March 1982 if higher) and any indexation allowance.

To establish how much of the overall gain can attract retirement relief, it is apportioned using the following formula:

$$\text{Overall gain} \times \frac{\text{Market value of the chargeable business assets}}{\text{Market value of \textbf{all} chargeable assets}}$$

10

The result of this calculation establishes the gain on which relief may be due (the balance of the gain being taxable). Whether this gain will be fully extinguished depends on the amount of retirement relief available by virtue of the taxpayer's ability to satisfy the conditions outlined above for ten years. The maximum possible relief is £150,000 plus one half of the gains up to £600,000 (see above and the case study at end of this chapter).

Gifting of shares

What happens where the person retiring decides to gift the shares instead of selling them?

All of the above principles apply with the overall gain being calculated and the available retirement relief (restricted to the gains attributable to chargeable business assets) deducted.

Any part of the gain, relating to **business assets only**, which now remains chargeable may be the subject of a claim for what is known as gift holdover relief. Under these arrangements the donor and the donee can jointly claim to have any gain arising (on **business** assets) held over. The result of this is that the donee takes the shares over (for future CGT purposes) at their MV at the date of transfer, less any gain which would otherwise have been taxable. When the donee eventually sells the shares the held over gain will crystallise, since the base cost being used has been reduced by this gain.

The Inheritance Tax (IHT) implications of such a gift must not be overlooked. A brief summary of the position is as follows:

- The gift of the shares will not attract an immediate inheritance tax liability since it will be regarded as a Potentially Exempt Transfer (PET). IHT may become payable if the donor fails to survive seven years after the gift (in which case a portion of the IHT will be payable depending on how long the donor survives).
- The amount which will be considered as a PET will be reduced by up to 100 per cent as a result of a relief for IHT known as business property relief (BPR). The amount of the relief will depend on the size of the donor's holding of shares.
- Where the donor has no other transfers (gifts) during the year then the first £3,000 of any gift is exempt. If he had no transfers in the previous tax year then a £6,000 exemption will be available this year.
- Where IHT becomes payable, the full rate is 40 per cent on the value of an estate in excess of £150,000 (the nil rate band).

Impact of taxation on business disposal

This chapter has demonstrated that there are a number of taxation matters to consider when an individual decides to dispose of a business and a phrase which has been often used in this context is that the taxpayer should 'plan to cease, rather than cease to plan'. The three main areas where taxation could have a serious impact on an individual who sells a business are now summarised:

Capital gains tax

As we have seen in this chapter, substantial gains can arise on the disposal. Where the individual is retiring at the age of 55, retirement relief can substantially mitigate this gain. Where the business has been run as a partnership or a sole trader, there is usually no difficulty in establishing eligibility for the relief. However, where shares in a family company are being sold, great care must be taken to ensure that the seller qualifies for relief, in terms of his shareholding, at the date of retirement. Where an individual does not qualify, by reason of age or by failing to have the appropriate shareholding, the CGT will be payable on the whole gain (less an annual exemption of £5,800).

Income tax

Where a business which is not a company is being sold and, therefore, ceasing to trade, then the assessment rules for cessation (see Chapter 3) can result in substantially increased assessments for the two years prior to cessation. Great care is required in choosing the optimum cessation date. These problems do **not** arise where shares in a company are being sold.

Capital allowances

When a non-company business is terminated, the assets are being sold and this can give rise to a claw back of capital allowances previously given, in the form of balancing charges (see Chapter 4). These balancing charges are regarded as taxable income in the tax year of the cessation and can give rise to substantial tax bills. It is in the interest of persons selling a business to ensure that the breakdown of the selling price of a business does not overstate the value of assets which could give rise to balancing charges. It would be helpful if more of the selling price could be allocated to those assets, such as goodwill, which will give rise to capital gains which could be mitigated by retirement relief. It is absolutely vital that the formal offer to purchase the business shows **clearly** the breakdown of the price to be paid. Not all solicitors appreciate the importance of this point and, before accepting any offer, a seller should show it to his tax adviser. The form of offer which states that the allocation of the purchase price 'will be mutually agreed between the parties' should be avoided at all costs as this can lead to disputes which can drag on for months!

Readers should obtain a copy of the Inland Revenue publication CGT 6 – *Capital Gains Tax – Retirement relief on disposal of a business.*

Case study

This short case study will illustrate the points made in this chapter.

Paisley Ltd had the following assets at 31 December 1992:

Buildings	£180,000
Goodwill	60,000
Fixed Plant and Machinery	20,000
Investments in other companies (not in same trade)	40,000
Stock	60,000
Debtors	30,000
Bank	10,000

Mr Paul is a full time working director of the company and is aged 57. He holds 35% of the ordinary shares which he acquired on 1 January 1984 at a cost of £80,000. On 1 January 1993 he retires and disposes of his entire holding for £130,000.

1. Compute the chargeable gain arising.

2. What would the position be if he gifted the shares to a nephew?

3. What would the retirement relief have been had the disposal price been £300,000?

Solution

Mr Paul qualifies for retirement relief since he owns 35% of the shares (more than 25%) and he is aged 57.

He has been in a qualifying position for **nine** years and will thus receive 9/10 only of the maximum relief.

The computation would proceed:

Proceeds		£130,000
Less cost	£80,000	
Indexation say	12,000	
		92,000
Overall gain		£ 38,000
Portion of gain attracting retirement relief: $£38{,}000 \times \frac{180+60+20}{180+60+20+40} =$		£ 32,933
Less, retirement relief: 9/10 × £150,000		135,500
		Nil
Balance of gain (£38,000 – 32,933)		5,067
Taxable gain		£ 5,067

1. The annual exemption of £5,800 would mean that no capital gains tax would be payable.

Mr Paul has used only £32,933 of his potential retirement relief and if, in the future, he was again in a position to claim retirement relief (in respect of a future disposal) he would potentially have available relief of £150,000 – £32,933 plus one half of the balance of any gains up to £600,000. This would of course be dependent on him satisfying the qualifying time period in a future business.

2. Had Mr Paul gifted the shares to his nephew, no gift holdover could be claimed in respect of the above gain of £5,067 since this part of the gain relates to non-business assets. Only where, after retirement relief, there remain taxable gains arising from business assets (using the apportionment basis in the case of a share transaction) can holdover relief be claimed.

Mr Paul would, therefore, be assessed to CGT on £5,067 (subject to the annual exemption of £5,800 if not used) and his nephew would acquire the shares at a cost, for CGT purposes, of £130,000.

Had the shares been gifted by Mr Paul in circumstances where he could **not** claim retirement relief, then the above gain of £32,933 could have been the subject of a claim for holdover relief, reducing his nephew's base cost for CGT to £97,067 (£130,000 – £32,933).

3 Had the disposal price of the shares been £300,000, then the calculations would have been as follows:

Overall gain (£300,000 – £92,000)			£208,000
Qualifying for retirement relief:			
$£208{,}000 \times \dfrac{180+60+20}{180+60+20+40} =$			£180,267
Less Retirement relief: 9/10 × £150,000		£135,000	
One half relief band:			
Excess of gains over £135,000 (£180,267 – £135,000) =	£45,267		
Maximum on which one half given:			
9/10 × £450,000 =	£405,000		
Relief = one half of lower figure 1/2 × £45,267		£ 22,634	
			£157,634
Chargeable gain			£ 22,633
Balance of gain (£208,000 – £180,267)			27,733
Total chargeable gain (subject to annual exemption if not used against other gains in year)			£ 50,366

If the shares were gifted, the donee's base cost for CGT would become:

MV of shares at transfer	£300,000
Less, holdover relief (gain on business assets)	22,633
	£277,367

The balance of the gain, £27,733 would be assessed on Mr Paul.

---

11 Tax mitigation for owners of businesses

Reducing the income tax burden □ Pension plans □ Share Option Schemes □ The Business Expansion Scheme (BES) □ Enterprise Zone Buildings □ Professional advice □ Checklist

In many books of this type dealing with taxation, there is often a chapter or section on what is described as 'tax planning'. The author's argument against this approach is that this part of the book is often presented as a free standing chapter, invariably separated from the information needed to understand the 'plan' being put forward by several pages. This requires the unsophisticated reader to constantly refer back to the appropriate chapter containing the information dealing with the 'plan', and often to become thoroughly confused!

The approach taken in this book has been to include any inherent planning opportunities in each of the chapters as the book has progressed, so that the 'plan' is presented to the reader when the background information is still fresh in the mind. For example, Chapter 3 dealt with basis of assessment rules, and then explored the use of optimum cessation dates; Chapter 5, dealing with partnerships, considered the effects of changes of partners; and Chapter 7, dealing with companies, contrasted companies with other forms of trading as well as considering dividends versus salary as a means of extracting cash. So almost all of what could be described as 'tax planning' has already been covered! A brief reminder of these areas will be given in the form of a checklist at the end of this chapter.

In this chapter it is the intention to look at those ways in which the tax burden of a business and of the owners of businesses can be reduced by using the opportunities on offer within the legislation. It will not address the type of tax planning involving 'artificial' transactions which have received short shrift in the courts in recent years. So this chapter will examine the means by which the owners of businesses can reduce their personal tax bills (either arising from their income from the business or otherwise) and in some cases reduce the tax burden of the business.

Reducing the income tax burden

Here we are essentially talking about 'sheltering' income from taxation – to use the technical terminology. There are rather more opportunities to shelter income than there are for capital gains. In the latter case, while CGT may be postponed (rollover and holdover reliefs) the only real 'shelter' is retirement relief) apart from capital losses).

In the case of income there are four major ways of reducing tax:

- the use of pension plans
- the use of share options in companies
- investments in the Business Expansion Scheme (BES)
- investments in Enterprise Zone Buildings

The first of these, the use of pension plans, is the most obvious means of tax reduction for both individuals and businesses and much of the remainder of this chapter will examine the possibilities. The second, share options, have possibly limited applications in very small companies, but can be extremely tax efficient once the company has grown. The other two, BES and Enterprise Zone buildings, are really for those individuals who have significant taxable incomes and can afford to make substantial investments. The BES, however, is to end on 31 December 1993.

Pension plans

There are basically two types of pension arrangements, a scheme run by an employer, referred to as an Occupational Pension Scheme, and a Personal Pension Plan.

The former involves the employer setting the scheme up (with an insurance company) and it provides benefits for the employees in the form of a lump sum on retirement plus a pension. It will also, generally, provide life assurance cover for employees. Personal pension plans can be taken out by individuals who are employees not in an occupational scheme or by persons who are self-employed.

There have been a number of significant changes in the taxation provisions relating to pension plans in recent years and it is not intended, in this book, to deal with any of the special rules applying to schemes set up prior to July 1988.

Whatever type of scheme is involved any investment made in

it will probably be the most tax efficient move that a business person will ever make! There are three tax efficient aspects:

- tax relief on the amounts invested (subject to limits)
- the pension fund grows free from **all** taxation
- there will be a tax free lump sum at maturity (subject to limits)

Personal Pension Plans

Since this book is intended for business owners, the coverage will be restricted to the use of such plans by self-employed persons i.e. sole traders and partners. Employees can individually take out such plans without involving their employers. Employees who are directors are unlikely to be involved in this type of plan (using an occupational scheme instead).

Self-employed persons are able to contribute, and obtain tax relief on, a maximum percentage of their 'net relevant earnings' (NRE) each tax year. The percentage allowed depends on the person's age as shown in the following table:

Age on 6 April	*% of NRE (see below)*
35 or under	17.5
36–45	20
46–50	25
51–55	30
56–60	35
61 or over	40

The maximum NRE on which the above percentages can be claimed is currently £75,000 each tax year.

NRE consists of:

The amount **assessed** for the tax year (**Note:** on a preceding year basis)		£
Plus any Balancing charges (capital allowances)		£
Less, Capital allowances claimed	£	
Trading Losses	£	
		£
Net Relevant Earnings		£

11

The deduction of losses above is most important. Before claiming loss relief, particularly losses carried back in a new business, care should be taken where the loss relief claimed may displace relief already given for pensions contributions in that year.

The carry forward facility

There is one particular aspect of this form of relief which is extremely attractive and tax efficient, especially for those who have been in business for some time and are now, for the first time, considering a personal pension plan. This is the carry forward facility and it works as follows.

Where, in any of the previous **six** years of assessment, the full percentage of NRE has not been used up by pension contributions, then the aggregate of any unused element can form the basis for a single payment in the current tax year to give tax relief at the taxpayer's highest rate.

This facility is now illustrated using information relating to a taxpayer who is under 35 for the period shown:

Tax year	*NRE*	*17.5%*	*Premium paid*	*Unused relief*
1986/87	£ 6,000	£1,050	Nil	£1,050
1987/88	8,000	1,400	Nil	1,400
1988/89	12,000	2,100	Nil	2,100
1989/90	16,000	2,800	£500	2,300
1990/91	4,000	700	Nil	700
1991/92	6,000	1,050	Nil	1,050
Total unused relief				£8,600

If the NRE for 1992/93 is £35,000, then the taxpayer could make a single payment DURING 1992/93 on which full tax relief would be given of:

17.5% × £35,000	=	£ 6,125
Plus unused relief above		8,600
		£14,725

Much of this would save tax at 40%.

Unused relief can be brought forward for any years prior to the commencement of the trade, but not generally where the taxpayer was a member of an occupational scheme run by an employer.

The carry back system

You will note from the above that once unused relief becomes more than six years old, it drops out and is lost (the relief is used up on a first in first out basis). There is a facility which can extend the period. This is the carry back system, which allows the taxpayer to treat a payment made in one tax year as 'belonging' for tax purposes to the previous year. This claim must be made to the tax office within three months of the end of the tax year in which the payment was made.

Pension and lump sum payable

The pension, and the lump sum, available at the date of retirement (which can be as early as 50 years of age) will depend on how successfully the contributions have been invested. There is always the risk that the retirement date could coincide with the collapse in share prices – like 19th October 1987!

There is, therefore, no limit on the amount of pension payable but the lump sum cannot exceed one quarter of the value of the fund at retirement. The only other limit imposed on personal pension plans is that the contributions must be based on a maximum figure which, as indicated, stands at £75,000. This figure will be increased each year in line with inflation.

Premiums

A word of caution regarding when, and how much, to invest in a personal pension plan. Remember that the percentage calculation is based on the amount of profits **assessed** for the tax year **during** which the premiums are paid (apart from the carry back facility). Also remember the peculiar method of assessing new businesses. If we now put these two ideas together the point will become clear.

A taxpayer, aged 30, commenced business on 1 January 1992 and made the following profits:

Year ended 31 December 1992	£ 1,200
Year ended 31 December 1993	30,000
Year ended 31 December 1994	60,000

The position as far as pension contributions are concerned becomes:

Tax year	*Assessment*	*Maximum premium (17.5%)*
1991/92	£ 300	£ 52.50
1992/93	1,200	210.00
1993/94	1,200	210.00
1994/95	30,000	5,250.00
1995/96	60,000	10,500.00

Some pension personnel can be very persuasive – just be sure they understand the above provisions. Also, you should be aware that if you pay a very large premium sometime during 1993/94 when you are earning £30,000/£60,000 (and therefore can **afford** the premium) you will get tax relief on £210 **only**! Excess premiums **cannot** be carried forward but will be repaid.

For employees who are not members of an employer's occupational scheme the rules are similar. Their NRE will consist of their salary plus benefits rather than profits. Their contributions are paid net of basic rate income tax, whereas self-employed persons pay the premiums gross. Inland Revenue leaflet IR 78, *Personal Pensions*, will provide useful information.

Occupational Pension Schemes

These are schemes set up by an employer and run, on their behalf, by an insurance company.

The taxation advantages of running such a scheme are broadly similar to those enjoyed by Personal Pensions Schemes, although certain limits are placed on contributions and more importantly, on the benefits available.

- The contributions by the employer are deductible in arriving at the business's taxable profit (with virtually no limits – unlike personal pension plans). (See coverage of limits below.)
- Contributions paid by the employer on behalf of employees are not treated as taxable income in the hands of the employee.
- Contributions paid by employees (up to a maximum of 15 per cent of earnings of £75,000 p.a.) are deductible in arriving at the employee's tax liability.
- The fund grows free of all taxation.

- A tax free lump sum can be paid on retirement (subject to a maximum figure (currently £112,500).
- Life assurance cover can be arranged for death in service providing a tax free lump sum for employees.

In order to obtain these tax advantages, the scheme must be approved by the Inland Revenue who can only approve schemes which satisfy the legislation. The main conditions to be satisfied are:

- **the main purpose of the scheme is to provide benefits to the employee or his dependants**
- **the employer must contribute to the scheme (employee contributions are not essential)**
- **any employee contributions are limited to 15 per cent of earnings up to a maximum of £75,000**
- **no return of employees contributions can be made except at the discretion of the Revenue.**

For approval the scheme must also require that:

- **benefits become payable no earlier than age 60 (55 for females) and no later than age 70 (for personal pension plans the minimum age is 50). The Revenue have discretion to lower these limits.**
- **the final pension does not exceed two-thirds of final remuneration – up to a maximum of two-thirds of £75,000 = £50,000**
- **the maximum lump sum is restricted to one and a half times final salary – up to a maximum of £75,000 = £112,500.**

For those employees in schemes at 14 March 1989 these limits are higher. The principal attraction of these schemes, particularly for small companies where the directors are perhaps the only employees, is that the limits of 17.5 per cent etc. which apply to personal pension plans, have no application for the **employer's** contribution. In most small companies, where the scheme is run for only the directors, very large sums indeed can be put into pension schemes – with no personal contributions being required by the directors.

Normally, a company will make equal annual contributions to the scheme but, in addition, may make one-off special contributions. This decision is normally taken towards the end of the financial year when it is known roughly what the profits are likely to be. Often the special contribution has the effect of wiping out the taxable profit (or indeed creating a trading loss!). Where the special contribution is exceptionally large, the Revenue may require the deduction, for taxation purposes, to be spread forward over a maximum of five years. It would take a **very** special contribution in a small company for this to apply!

It is also open to company directors to eschew an occupational scheme and arrange their own personal pension plan (and possibly setting up a company scheme to provide death in service benefits only). It depends on the age of the director and how much he can afford. Bear in mind that employers can contribute to a personal pension plan (but the aggregate paid must not exceed 17.5 per cent etc.). It may also be the case that the director is paying tax, and therefore getting relief, at 40 per cent. Contributions by a small company (profits up to £250,000) will get relief at only 25 per cent. The facility for retiring at the age of 50 may be attractive also. Each case must be looked at individually, with professional advice being sought.

While the text has concentrated on directors of small companies, it is of course open to the company to allow other members of staff to join the scheme, either as contributory or non-contributory members. Indeed, the existence of a good pension scheme is a persuasive factor in attracting and retaining high quality staff.

The inclusion of a spouse in the scheme

There is one further possibility open to sole traders or partners who employ their wives or husbands in the business. There is nothing to prevent the owner setting up an employee scheme for the spouse and making substantial contributions to it.

The amounts are **not** limited by the percentages applicable to personal pension schemes. The author can recall making this point to a group of small businessmen – that a wife who helps in the business should be paid and perhaps a pension arranged – when one of the audience asked, 'Does she need to know?'! Chauvinism still lurks!

Administration of the scheme

The final decision to be made is whether to use an insurance company to administer the scheme or to establish a self-administered scheme. This decision can only be taken with expert advice. In all matters relating to pensions, it is prudent to seek advice from an Independent Intermediary registered under the Financial Services Act.

A final cautionary note on pensions

The contents of this chapter have been based on the legislation in force following the enactment of the Finance Act 1990. There have been numerous changes in this area in recent years and readers should be familiar with the law in force at the date of reading before proceeding. Recent events have suggested that problems relating to pension funds are not limited to the area of taxation!

Share Option Schemes

One of the other methods of rewarding directors and staff mentioned at the start of this chapter was the use of what are known as 'Share Option Schemes'. These are available only in companies and there are variations on this theme – Share Options and Profit Sharing Schemes (SAYE).

This book is aimed at rather small businesses which are sometimes run as companies and it is unlikely that such schemes will have much relevance to these companies at this stage in their development. Such companies will still be learning to walk – and it is not proposed to get them to run at this stage! Once the company has grown, it is certainly an extremely tax efficient method of rewarding staff, particularly the SAYE Share Option Scheme.

One of the initial difficulties with small companies is that their shares are unquoted and, in order to run option schemes, a value of the shares must be agreed. This can be expensive and time-consuming.

Readers who would like to find out more are referred to the excellent publications issued by most firms of accountants and to the series of leaflets issued by the Revenue, listed at the end of this chapter.

The Business Expansion Scheme (BES)

Under this arrangement (which is to cease on 31 December 1993), an individual, resident in the UK (but **not** a company), can obtain relief from tax at his highest rate on an investment of up to £40,000 per annum in certain types of companies. For those paying the higher rate of tax and with high disposable incomes, it can be very tax efficient. There are, however, risks since the companies involved are unquoted and can sometimes get into serious difficulties, resulting in the loss of all of the investor's cash!

There are broadly two sets of conditions which must be satisfied for the relief to be given – one concerning the investor and one concerning the company.

To qualify, an individual (or his associates) must not be:

- **an employee or partner of the company**
- **a director of the company who receives remuneration from the company during its first five years. Reimbursed expenses incurred by a director do not count as remuneration.**
- **the owner (with his associates) of more than 30 per cent of the company's ordinary shares (or share plus loan capital)**

'Associates' consist of spouses, antecedents, descendants and business partners but, curiously, not brothers or sisters.

The type of companies which qualify is not really of importance to the investor, since those which do not qualify will not be issuing prospectuses under the BES! However, it is often the case that small unquoted companies can use the tax advantages conferred on investors to attract funds through a BES scheme. The company's shares must not be dealt with on the Stock Exchange or the Unlisted Securities Market. The main types of small business which are excluded from the scheme are:

- dealing in land or shares
- leasing or hiring
- dealing in financial investments
- providing legal or accountancy services

This is not an exhaustive list and an obvious first step for a company contemplating a scheme is to check if the business qualifies! A considerable amount of work is involved in setting the scheme up and expert guidance must be obtained. The maximum amount which can be raised under the scheme is £750,000 (the promoter's fees can knock a hole in this!) unless the business is either shipping or the provision of properties under the assured tenancy arrangments, when the limit is £5M. Where more than half of a company's assets consist of land or buildings, the maximum amount allowed to be raised under the BES is £50,000 per annum.

Where the individual and the company satisfy the conditions, the individual can claim relief for an investment in **new** shares in the company of up to £40,000 each tax year (there is a minimum investment in each company of £500 p.a. – unless the investment is through a BES fund run by a financial institution). The relief can be claimed once the company has been trading for four months and the claim must be made within two years.

The promoter of the scheme will issue a BES certificate (Form BES 3) which should be completed and sent to your tax office. Provided the investor retains the shares for at least five years, the relief given cannot be withdrawn and if the shares are sold after this period, no CGT charge arises on any gain made.

Some or all of the relief may be withdrawn if the shares are sold within five years and any gain made will be chargeable to CGT. The relief will also be withdrawn if the company **ceases** to satisfy the qualifying conditions within **three years**.

Enterprise Zone Buildings

Certain areas of the UK which have suffered as a result of industrial decline, have been granted the designation of **Enterprise Zones**. In order to encourage investment in such areas, a package of incentives has been made available to those setting up businesses or providing investment for such purposes during the first 10 years of a Zone's life. Full details of the incentives for business owners considering setting up in such an area (or moving to one) can be obtained from your local enterprise agency (or company).

The main attraction for the provider of capital is that an allowance of 100 per cent of the cost of industrial or commercial buildings in the Zone is available. The investment opportunity is available to both companies and individuals and the relief can either be claimed in full in the year of investment, or a lesser amount can be claimed in the first year and the balance claimed in future years at the rate of 25 per cent per annum on the original cost of the building until the cost has been fully claimed.

This type of investment is heavily advertised in all the financial journals and there should be no difficulty in finding advice!

Professional advice

Other possible tax efficient opportunities which might be raised with a professional adviser include such things as Personal Equity Plans (PEPs) and Tax Exempt Special Savings Accounts (TESSAs).

In all investment matters it is vital that you are guided by your professional advisers who should be registered as Independent Financial Advisers under the Financial Services Act. This will provide some protection.

The following Inland Revenue publications should be obtained:

- IR 51 *The Business Expansion Scheme* (with IR 85 Private rented housing)
- IR 78 *Personal Pension Plans*
- IR 89 *Personal Equity Plans (PEPs)*
- IR 95 *Shares for employees – Profit sharing schemes*
- IR 97 *Shares for employees – SAYE share options*
- IR 99 *Shares for employees – Executive share options*

Checklist

Tax planning aspects covered in this book

Question	*Reference*
Which business expenses are tax deductible?	Chapter 2
Which accounting date should be chosen?	Chapter 3
When should the business cease trading or convert to a company?	Chapter 3
Which items of equipment etc. attract capital allowances?	Chapter 4
When should capital expenditure be incurred?	Chapter 4
Should machinery be bought or leased?	Chapter 4
What happens on a change of partners and can this save tax?	Chapter 5
How can loss relief be maximised?	Chapter 6
Should the business be run as a company?	Chapters 1 and 7
Should a spouse be a director?	Chapter 7
Should dividends be paid rather than salaries?	Chapter 7

Can gains arising on transferring a business to a company be mitigated?	Chapter 8
Can alternative methods of rewarding employees achieve savings?	Chapter 9
Can CGT bills be reduced on retirement?	Chapter 10
Can the shares be passed on as gifts free of taxes?	Chapter 10
How should the share capital of a small company be organised?	Chapter 10
How can tax be saved by using pension plans?	Chapter 11
Are there other tax efficient ways in which companies and individuals can invest surplus funds?	Chapter 11

12 Value Added Tax (VAT)

Registration for VAT □ VAT accounting systems

This final chapter will cover briefly the impact of the VAT system on the small business. For fuller coverage the reader is referred to the excellent companion book in the NatWest Small Business Bookshelf series, *Understanding VAT* by William Lovell and reference will be made to this book from time to time.

The VAT system requires registered traders to charge VAT on all taxable supplies of goods and services ('output VAT') and to remit it, after deducting VAT suffered on their own purchases and expenses ('input VAT'), to Customs and Excise within 30 days of the end of each quarterly period. Where the input VAT suffered is more than the output VAT charged, a repayment will be made by Customs and Excise. Where this is a regular occurrence, the trader can have a monthly settlement period rather than three monthly, thus improving cash flow.

This latter point about cash flow is central to the operation of the VAT system and sometimes traders can get into serious difficulties through failing to control the position. It is common to hear traders say, 'I have a large VAT bill to pay and it is killing my business'. This approach is based on the mistaken view that the VAT to be paid to Customs and Excise (C & E) is an **additional** cost to the business. It is not, but it can have a devastating effect on the cash flow for the financially undisciplined! The point is that the money being paid to C & E **never belonged** to the business and represents cash collected on behalf of the government which has to be paid over at the appropriate time. By that time, the money has very often been spent or debtors have been slow in paying.

One way round this problem is for the trader to lodge, in a separate (perhaps a deposit) bank account a proportion of the takings or cash collected from debtors and to regard this money as 'belonging' to C & E and, therefore, not available for spending in the business. VAT bills can then be settled without upsetting the cash flow position. Any interest earned is a bonus – but subject to income or corporation tax!

Registration for VAT

When?

Now to the question of registration and the first obvious question which arises is – when is registration required?

The Finance Act 1990 introduced a new regime for registration which is rather more user friendly than the previous system. A trader is required to register, by notifying C & E, within 30 days of the end of any 12 month period where the **taxable turnover** (i.e. sales – **not** profit) has exceeded the annual registration limit – currently £36,600. Exceptionally, registration is required at any time where the anticipated turnover in the **next 30 days** is likely to exceed the **annual** registration limit – most unlikely in small businesses.

This new approach requires the trader to monitor most carefully his turnover as each successive month ends and to calculate, at the end of **each month**, the total for the previous **12 months**.

Failure to register within the permitted time period can result in penalties, as can most breaches of the system. These penalties are set out in *Understanding VAT*, and should be taken very seriously.

It should be noted that the turnover is described as the 'taxable' turnover. Many traders often get into difficulties as a result of failing to appreciate what this means. This stems from an unusual feature of the UK VAT system – there are two rates of tax – 15 per cent and zero per cent! In other words, items which are 'zero' rated are still regarded as 'taxable' and **must be included** in arriving at the annual turnover. The confusion is not helped by the trader's inability to distinguish between 'zero' rated items – which are taxable supplies – and 'exempt' items – which are outwith the scope of VAT. These again are listed in *Understanding VAT* (and in the VAT publications available from C & E).

This means that those businesses dealing wholly or mainly in zero rated items – possibly food – must register where the turnover exceeds the annual limit. Where sales consist *wholly* of zero-rate items, a trader may request exemption from registration.

The consequences

The next question is – what are the consequences of being registered? Registration imposes a number of requirements on the trader:

- the need to issue full VAT invoices to customers (less full invoices may be issued in certain types of businesses where the value is less than £50).
- the need to maintain records of a standard which satisfies C & E showing clearly how any VAT paid to, or recovered from, C & E has been calculated.
- the need to submit the business records to the inspection of VAT officers who will visit you from time to time.
- the need to submit quarterly (or monthly) returns within the permitted time period (with penalties for late returns).

All of these requirements are covered fully in *Understanding VAT*.

Pros and cons of registration

The question which follows on from the above is, even if the turnover is **less** than the annual registration limit, **should** the business register?

The first point to make is that registration brings with it all the above requirements, which you may feel are unacceptable. However, there is no barrier to registration in these circumstances and the positive aspects should be considered.

It may be useful to compare the effect of registration with non-registration, using figures to illustrate the difference.

Example

Consider a trader buying an item for £200 and selling it for £300 (both items vattable) and see what the respective positions would be:

	Not registered		*Registered*		
Selling price		£300		£300	
Add, VAT charged		–		52.50	(collected and held for up to 4 months)
Total selling price		300		352.50	
Cost price	£200		£200		
VAT paid	35		35		
		235		235	
Net cash inflow		£ 65		£117.50	

With registration the cash flow is improved by £52.50 – VAT charged. In addition the registered trader will not have to account for the VAT until up to four months later, at which time he will remit to C & E:

Output VAT	£52.50
Less, Input VAT	35.00
	£17.50

The respective profits positions are:

	Not registered		*Registered*
Sales value	£300		£300
Less, cost (including VAT)	235	(excluding VAT)	200
Net profit	65		100

The difference is, of course, due to the fact that the registered trader was able to recover the input VAT, whereas for the non-registered trader the input VAT was an additional, unavoidable cost.

The one other occasion on which voluntary registration may appear attractive is at the *start* of a business. This is because at that time the business will probably be spending heavily on equipment, signs, motor vans or lorries which all carry substantial amounts of input VAT, which, if repaid to the business would dramatically improve the cash position. While this is certainly attractive, you must remember that you cannot opt into the system for a few quarters then opt out again once you have got your repayments. It may take slightly longer to get out! It should be noted that input tax may not be claimed on the purchase of private cars. However capital allowances, where appropriate, may be claimed on the VAT inclusive cost of the car.

VAT accounting schemes

There are two remaining aspects of VAT which will be a great interest to small businesses:

- The cash accounting scheme
- Annual accounting

The Cash Accounting Scheme

Where a trader's annual taxable turnover does not exceed £300,000 (which should include many reading this book) then the trader may apply to C & E for permission to operate this scheme.

It is particularly attractive for those businesses selling on credit since, in such businesses, output VAT must normally be accounted for in the quarter in which the sale is **made** (not when the cash is collected). The essential feature of this scheme is that a trader is not required to account for output VAT until the quarter in which the cash is **collected** from the debtor. This can clearly improve cash flow and in addition, provides automatic relief for bad debts – if you do not collect the cash, you do not pay over the VAT charged.

If you are in this scheme, input VAT on purchases and expenses must also be dealt with on a cash basis.

Annual accounting

The final area of interest is the annual accounting scheme. This is analogous to running a budget account for say, gas or electricity bills, where fixed regular payments (based on previous experience) are made during the year, with a squaring up to be done at the year end.

The trader estimates his turnover for the ensuing year and makes nine monthly payments by direct debit. Apart from smoothing out cash flow, it has the attraction that only one VAT return is required each year – due two months after the end of the year. As in the cash accounting scheme, the turnover limit is £300,000 p.a.

Any other VAT problems encountered by traders, including the use of the special scheme used by different types of traders, are fully covered in the companion book referred to at the beginning of this chapter, *Understanding VAT*.

Appendix: Income Tax – rates and allowances 1992/93

Taxable income	*Rate*
First £2,000	20%
Next £25,000	25%
Balance	40%

Note: Capital gains are taxed at an individual's highest rate of income tax.

Main reliefs and allowances	£
Persons under 65	
Personal allowance	3,445
Married couple's allowance	1,720
Persons aged 65 to 74	
Personal allowance	4,200
Married couple's allowance	2,465
Persons aged over 75	
Personal allowance	4,370
Married couple's allowance	2,505
Income limit for age allowance	14,200

Other reliefs	
Additional relief for single parents	1,720
Widow's bereavement allowance	1,720
Blind person	1,080

Index

Related titles in the NatWest Business Handbooks

Book-keeping and Accounting
Geoffrey Whitehead

The emphasis in this key title is to allow specific techniques to be used: from drawing up an opening balance sheet, through transaction recording, to bank reconciliation and preparation of final accounts. It is clearly written and explained with many examples.

Coverage includes:

- VAT, with special emphasis on VAT for retailers
- proprietary book-keeping systems, e.g. Simplex, Kalamazoo and FinCo
- information on computerised systems

Published 1989, 256 pages, Paper

Small Business Finance

John C Lambden and David Targett

A case study-based book which shows the reader how to assess the 'financial viability' of a business idea.

It provides a thorough understanding of break-even and cash-flow and goes on to build up a case for start-up and for development finance, with practical advice on proposals and business plans to bank managers or financiers.

Published 1990, 128 pages, Paper

Understanding VAT
William Lovell
VAT is perhaps the tax most feared and least understood by small traders and company owners. This book explains both the basic principles and complexities of VAT in a very readable and entertaining style. It is designed to make the administration of VAT less of a burden to smaller business by illuminating the reasoning behind the notices and leaflets issued with increasing frequency by the government, which could be subtitled 'or what the VATman didn't tell you'. Small business owners and managers whose trading is expanding over the threshold limit (£23,600), either sole traders, partnerships or limited companies, accountants and financial advisers will find this text particularly appealing.

Published 1990, 176 pages, Paper